Learning to
Program in C

ALSO AVAILABLE

(By the same author)

BP232 A Concise Introduction to MS-DOS

BP243 BBC-BASIC86 on Amstrad PCs & IBM Compatibles
Book 1 - Language[1]

BP244 BBC-BASIC86 on Amstrad PCs & IBM Compatibles
Book 2 - Graphics and Disk Files[1]

BP250 Programming in FORTRAN 77

BP259 A Concise Introduction to UNIX

BP260 A Concise Introduction to OS/2

BP261 A Concise Introduction to Lotus 1-2-3

BP264 A Concise Advanced User's Guide to MS-DOS

BP274 A Concise Introduction to SuperCalc5

BP270 A Concise Introduction to Symphony[2]

BP279 A Concise Introduction to Excel

BP283 A Concise Introduction to SmartWare II[3]

BP284 Programming in QuickBASIC

BP288 A Concise Introduction to Windows 3.0

BP294 A Concise Introduction to Microsoft Works[2]

BP302 A Concise User's Guide to Lotus 1-2-3 Release 3.1[2]

BP314 A Concise Introduction to Quattro Pro 3.0

BP318 A Concise User's Guide to MS-DOS 5

BP319 Making MS-DOS Work for You[2]

BP325 A Concise User's Guide to Windows 3.1

[1]co-author Keith Thompson
[2]co-author Phil Oliver
[3]co-author Steve Cant

Learning to Program in C

by

Noel Kantaris

BERNARD BABANI (publishing) LTD.
THE GRAMPIANS
SHEPHERDS BUSH ROAD
LONDON W6 7NF
ENGLAND

PLEASE NOTE

Although every care has been taken with the production of this book to ensure that any projects, designs, modifications and/or programs, etc., contained herewith, operate in a correct and safe manner and also that any components specified are normally available in Great Britain, the Publishers and Author(s) do not accept responsibility in any way for the failure (including fault in design) of any project, design, modification or program to work correctly or to cause damage to any equipment that it may be connected to or used in conjunction with, or in respect of any other damage or injury that may be so caused, nor do the Publishers accept responsibility in any way for the failure to obtain specified components.

Notice is also given that if equipment that is still under warranty is modified in any way or used or connected with home-built equipment then that warranty may be void.

© 1989, © 1993 BERNARD BABANI (publishing) LTD

First Published — January 1989
Reprinted — April 1990
Reprinted — March 1991
Reprinted — January 1992
Reprinted — October 1992
Revised Edition — March 1993
Reprinted — January 1994

British Library Cataloguing in Publication Data:

Kantaris, Noel
    Learning to Program in C
    1. Computer systems. Programming languages:
    I. Title
    005.13'3

ISBN 0 85934 203 4

Printed and Bound in Great Britain by Cox & Wyman Ltd, Reading

PREFACE

C is a highly portable general purpose language which is structured, modular and compiled. It was written by Dennis Ritchie in the early 1970s to support the development of the UNIX operating system. C is the result of a development process that started with a language called BCPL (Basic Combined Programming Language) which was developed from CPL (an earlier language), by Martin Richards in 1967 as a compiler writing tool. In turn, BCPL influenced a language called B, which was developed by Ken Thompson and which finally led to the creation of C in the 1970s.

For many years, the de facto standard for C was described in *The C Programming Language* by Brian Kernigham and Dennis Ritchie (Prentice-Hall, 1978) and as supplied with the UNIX version 5 operating system. As such, C was used originally for systems programming, but as UNIX became one of the most popular multi-user operating systems, 85% of the code of which is written in C, the language has been adopted by programmers for almost any programming task. In 1983, a committee was formed to work on the creation of an ANSI standard that would define C completely. By 1987 the proposed standard was being adopted by all manufacturers of C compilers.

Most people are familiar with Basic, which is not a very efficient computer language. A separate program called the *Basic interpreter*, interprets each and every statement of a Basic program every time it encounters it, into the machine code the particular computer can understand. Although lately Basic compilers have been made available, they tend to be specific to a given Basic dialect which itself is associated with a particular computer. Thus, Basic code is slow in execution, and one computer's Basic differs considerably from that of another.

Traditionally, those who needed to write fast execution programs, used to resort to writing in Assembler. However, programming in Assembler is a very tedious and slow process and has the added disadvantage of being different on different computers, thus making such programs almost impossible to transfer from one computer to another. Amongst the many languages that overcome the above limitations (Fortran, Cobol, Pascal, C, etc), C is by far the most up and coming language of today.

C is a structured language some features of which are to be found in some other popular languages running on IBM compatibles, such as Pascal and Fortran 77, particularly in the area of control of program flow. Programs can be written in modular form which when compiled provide the building blocks for larger and more complicated applications. A separate program, the C compiler, is used to generate the machine specific code that will actually be executed by the particular computer. This means, of course, that instead of having to learn to program several computers in their own specific language such as Assembler or some dialect of Basic, you only need to learn to program in C.

C combines elements of high-level languages with the functionalism of assembler. For example, C supports the concept of data types just as other high-level languages, but it is not a strongly typed language like, say, Pascal. On the other hand, C provides access to bitwise operations and the manipulation of bytes and addresses, as well as allowing the storage of variables in registers for more efficient and fast code - operations that normally are restricted to assembly language programming. Thus, if you intend to write programs that need to be compact, fast in execution, and yet transportable from one computer to another, then C is the language you should be using.

ABOUT THIS BOOK

This book is a guide to C programming. C statements are introduced and explained with the help of simple, but completely working programs. The user is encouraged to type these into the computer, save them, and keep improving them as more complex language statements and commands are encountered. Graded problems are set at the end of each chapter, some with financial or scientific bent, so that users can choose their own level of problem difficulty on which to practise with some additional choice in the preference of the field of application. Full working solutions appear at the back of the book.

Chapters 1-3 deal with the basic C statements which control program flow and allow the user to manage with most aspects of the language, with the result that most general problems can be solved easily and effectively. Chapters 4-5 introduce the concepts of string arrays, numeric arrays and function subprograms which expand the programming capabilities of the user beyond the beginner's level. Chapters 6 deals entirely with data-file handling on disc, while part of Chapter 7 deals with unique C structures, both of which should be of interest to all those who need to process large quantities of data.

ABOUT THE AUTHOR

Graduated in Electrical Engineering at Bristol University and after spending three years in the Electronics Industry in London, took up a Tutorship in Physics at the University of Queensland. Research interests in Ionospheric Physics, led to the degrees of M.E. in Electronics and Ph.D. in Physics. On return to the UK, he took up a Post-Doctoral Research Fellowship in Radio Physics at the University of Leicester, and in 1973 a Senior Lectureship in Engineering at The Camborne School of Mines, Cornwall, where since 1978 he has also assumed the responsibility of Head of Computing.

ACKNOWLEDGEMENTS

I would like to thank colleagues at the Camborne School of Mines for the helpful tips and suggestions which assisted me in the writing of this book.

TRADEMARKS

IBM is a registered trademark of International Business Machines Corporation

MS-DOS is a registered trademark of Microsoft Corporation

Turbo C is a registered trademark of Borland International

CONTENTS

1. **LANGUAGE OVERVIEW** 1
   Comment Lines 2
   The Function **main()** 2
   Variables and the Declaration Statement 2
      Table of C Keywords 4
   Type Conversion 4
   Constants and Expressions 5
      Constants 5
      Expressions 5
   The **printf** Function 6
   The **scanf** Function 6
   The Assignment Statement 6
   Compiling and Executing a Program 7
   Summary of Some C Rules 10
   Problems 10

2. **OPERATORS & I/O CONTROL** 11
   Arithmetic Operators 11
   Formatted Output 12
      Table of I/O Field Types 13
      Table of Escape Sequences 14
   Character I/O 15
   The % Operator in Integer Division 16
   Relational Operators 17
      Table of Relational Operators 17
   Logical Operators 17
   Ternary Operator 18
   Unary Operators 18
   Address Operators 19
   Bitwise Operators 20
      Table of Bitwise Operators 20
   Combined Operators 22
      Table of Priority of C Operators 23
   Problems 24

3. CONTROL OF PROGRAM FLOW 25
The if Statement 25
The if..else Statement 26
Nested if..else Statements 27
The while Loop 27
The do while Loop 28
The for loop 29
Nested Loops 32
Speeding up Loops by Using Registers 33
Unconditional Program Branching 33
   The goto Statement 33
   The continue Statement 34
   The break Statement 34
The switch Command 35
Problems 37

4. ARRAYS & POINTERS 39
Defining a String 39
   Character Array Definition 39
   Character Pointer Definition 41
Pointer Memory Allocation 41
String Arrays 43
   Table of ASCII Conversion Codes 46
String and Substring Manipulation 47
Subscripted Numerical Variables 49
The Bubble Sort Technique 51
   Table of String Functions 52
Problems 54

5. FUNCTIONS 55
Standard Arithmetic Functions 55
   sin(x), cos(x) and **tan(x)** 56
   asin(x), acos(x) and **atan(x)** 56
   hypot(x,y) 56
   sqrt(x) 56
   exp(x) 57
   log(x) and **log10(x)** 58
   abs(n), fabs(x) and **labs(x)** 58
   poly(x,n,c[]) 58
User-defined Functions 59

Pointers and Functions 62
   Pointers to Variables in Functions 62
   Pointers to Strings in Functions 63
   Pointers to Arrays in Functions 64
Recursion 65
Problems 68

6. **STREAMS & FILES** 69
Types of Streams and Files 69
   Table of Values of Mode 70
   Table of Common Library File Functions 71
Sequential Data Files 72
Command-line Arguments 73
Error and EOF Handling 74
File Read/Write Functions 75
File Scan/Print Functions 78
Random Access Files 80
Problems 86

7. **DEFINED DATA TYPES** 87
The typedef Keyword 87
Enumerated Data Types 87
Structures 89
Arrays of Structures 91
Unions 95
Bitfields 96
Linked Lists 97
Problem 98

APPENDIX A - THE ED LINE EDITOR 99
Invoking the **ed** Line Editor 99
   The Append Command 100
   The List Command 101
   The Write Command 101
   The Change Command 102
   The Insert Command on an Existing File 102
   The Delete Command 103
   The Move and Transcribe Commands 103
   The Search Command 103
   The Substitute Command 104
Exiting **ed** 105

APPENDIX B - SOLUTIONS TO PROBLEMS 107
Problem 1.1 107
Problem 1.2 107
Problem 2.1 108
Problem 2.2 108
Problem 3.1 109
Problem 3.2 110
Problem 4.1 111
Problem 4.2 112
Problem 5.1 113
Problem 5.2 114
Problem 6.1 115
Problem 6.2 116
Problem 7.1 118

INDEX 121

1. LANGUAGE OVERVIEW

C is a high level programming language which is easy to learn, but which remains extremely flexible. A program written in C, called the source program, is compiled into machine code, called the object code, which is very compact and executes extremely fast. If you are operating under the MS-DOS environment, you can enter a new C program in your computer with the use of either the full screen editor **Edit**, if you are a DOS 5 or higher user, or the line editor **edlin**, if you are a pre-DOS 5 user. If, on the other hand, you are operating under the UNIX environment, then you could use the **Ed** line editor which is fully explained in Appendix A. However, you could use a word processor to enter a C source file, provided it runs on the particular environment and is of a type that creates an ASCII file. Some implementations of C, such as Microsoft's and Borland's Turbo C, come with their own editor in an integrated package.

In what follows, it is assumed that your editor is evoked by typing the appropriate command followed by the filename. For example, to create a C source file called **average**, using UNIX's line editor **ed**, type

ed average.c   (followed by pressing <Enter>)

If the filename **average.c** does not already exist on the disc, the editor will inform you of the fact. A program to calculate the average of three numbers will have to be entered as follows:

```
/* CALCULATE AVERAGES */
main( )
{
    float a,b,c,d,average;

    printf("Enter three numbers: ");
    scanf("%f %f %f",&a,&b,&c);
    d=a+b+c;
    average=d/3.0;
    printf("The average is %f",average);
}
```

The above program is presented to give an overview of what a C source program is and how it is entered in the computer. All the C statements contained therein will be discussed in detail in the following pages. So, there is no need to worry!

1

Comment Lines

A C source program consists of *statements* (one per line) and *comment lines*. Comment lines are enclosed by the characters /* (at the start of the comment) and */ (at the end of the comment).

The Function main( )

Every C program must have a function called **main** which must appear only once in a program. The parentheses following the word **main** must be present, but there must be no parameters included (parameters will be explained later, when we discuss C functions). The main part of the program is enclosed within braces **{ }**, and consists of declaration statements, assignment statements and other C functions. In the above program there are six statements within the braces; a declaration statement (the first statement of the main program starting with the word **float**), two assignment statements (the fourth and fifth statements starting with the variable names **d** and **average**) and three function statements, two to print information on the screen and one to scan the keyboard for input.

As C is a free form language, the semi-colon (;) at the end of each line is a must. It acts as a statement terminator, telling the compiler where an instruction ends. Free form means that statements can be indented and blank lines inserted in the source file to improve readability, and statements can span several lines. However, each statement must be terminated with a semi-colon. If you forget to include the semi-colon, the compiler will produce an error, indicating the *next* line as the source of the error. This can cause some confusion, as the statement objected to can be correct, yet a syntax error is produced.

Variables and the Declaration Statement

A variable is a quantity that is referred to by name, such as **a**, **b**, **c**, **d** and **average** in the above program. A variable can take on many values during program execution, but you must make sure that they are given an initial value, as C does not do so automatically. However, before variables can be used in a program, they must be declared in a *type* declaration statement.

In C, a variable can be one of three distinct data types, **float**, **int** and **char**, with several additional qualifiers. The most common of these are listed on the next page:

2

float	for single precision floating point numbers, such as 3.33333. These are expressed in 32 bits and their range is $\pm3.4E\pm38$;
double	for double precision floating point numbers, which are twice as large as variables of type **float**, expressed in 64 bits within the range $\pm1.7E\pm308$;
int	for integer numbers, which are whole numbers without a decimal point, expressed in 16 bits within the range -32768 to 32767;
long	for long integer numbers, in 32 bits within the range -2147483648 to 2147483647;
char	for storing one byte or one ASCII character, which are any of the characters appearing on the keyboard. These are expressed in 8 bits and their range is -128 to 127;
unsigned int	unsigned integer numbers, expressed in 16 bits within the range 0 to 65535;
unsigned long	unsigned long integer numbers expressed in 32 bits within the range 0 to 4294967295;
unsigned char	unsigned character, expressed in 8 bits within the range 0 to 255.

Thus, before we can use any variable in a C program, we must declare its type (**float**, **double**, **int**, **long**, or **char**) and its name. Variable names can be of any length, but only the first *eight* characters are significant. Upper and lower case variables can be used, but it is traditional to use lower case for names of variables and upper case for names of constants (to be discussed shortly). Use of the underscore within variable names (for example, **x_value**) is permitted and can be used to improve readability.

C reserves a number of *keywords* for use as commands (listed on the next page) and these must not be used as variables.

Table of C Keywords

auto	double	int	struct
break	else	long	switch
case	num	register	typedef
char	extern	return	union
const	float	short	unsigned
continue	for	signed	void
default	goto	sizeof	volatile
do	if	static	while

Once variables have been declared and have values assigned to them, they can be used in assignment statements and/or expressions in the rest of the program to perform desired calculations. A variable must have a value before it is used in an expression or in the right hand side of an assignment statement.

Type Conversion
Sometimes certain operations require us to use a variable in a type-form other than the one it was declared in the *type* statement. For example, suppose variables **a**, **b**, **c** and **d**, of the previous program had been declared as integers, as follows:

```
main( )
{
    int a,b,c,d;
    float average;

    printf("Enter three numbers: ");
    scanf("%d %d %d",&a,&b,&c);
    d=a+b+c;
    average=d/3;
    printf("The average is %f",average);
}
```

If we then supplied the program with the values 1, 2 and 2, the value of d will be 5. The value of average will then be the integer division of 5/3 which is 1. Clearly this is wrong.

To overcome this, we can temporarily change the type of variable **d** to floating point by using the statement

```
average=(float)d/3;
```

which will result in the correct average value being calculated.

4

Similarly, a variable **x**, which was declared as a floating point variable in a declaration statement, can be changed temporarily to an integer by writing **(int)x**.

Also, note that C follows the convention of automatically converting an integer variable into floating point if it is used in an expression containing other floating point numbers. That is why we divided **d** by 3, rather than 3.0 in the previous program!

Constants and Expressions

Constants:

A constant is a quantity that either appears as a number (3.0 in the fifth statement in the main part of the AVERAGE program) or is referred to by name, but has only one value during program execution; that which was allocated to it. Constants can be *defined* via the **#define** statement which must appear before the **main( )** function.

Thus, a constant called **TOTAL** can be defined as follows:

```
#define TOTAL 3.0
main( )
{
    ---;
    ---;

    average=d/TOTAL;

    ---;
    ---;
}
```

Note the convention of using upper case letters for constants to distinguish them from variables. Also note that the hash sign (#) of the define statement must be in the first column of the line in which it appears. This and the placement of the **#include** statement (which will be discussed later) are the only restrictions to C's free-form statement entry.

Expressions:

An expression, when referred to in this text, implies a constant, a variable or a combination of either or both, separated by arithmetic operators (*, /, %, +, and –). Of the five arithmetic operators, only the symbol for modulus (which is the %) will be unfamiliar to the newcomer to the C language.

5

The printf Function

The **printf** function allows the printing of text to prompt the user to supply information as was done in the first **printf** statement of the AVERAGE program. Note that such text must be enclosed in full quotation marks ("). The function can also be used to print the result of a calculation, as was done on the second **printf** statement of the same program. This result is held in the variable named **average**.

Following the opening brackets of the **printf** function, there is information on what we intend to print out, enclosed in full quotation marks. The information was included in the program to make it easier for the user to identify the output. Note the **%f** which appears prior to the closing quotes; it informs the compiler that the variable **average** which follows, is to be printed in floating point format. Later we will discuss other formats which exist for both input and output (I/O) streams.

The scanf Function

The **scanf** function allows formatted input to be taken from the keyboard. Three **%f** formats (separated by a space and enclosed in quotes) inform the compiler that each of the three inputs are going to be floating point numbers. Also, note that **scanf** requires the arguments used in it to be *pointers* to the actual variables. Thus, **&a** holds the address in memory where the variable **a** is to be stored.

The space between the three **%f** format commands, used in the **scanf** function, indicates that the three corresponding variables will be entered with a *white* space in between them, that is, the numbers typed on the keyboard will be separated by a space (or any number of spaces), or by line feeds (which are created when pressing the <Enter> key after typing each numeric value). If we wanted to separate these numeric values with a comma (instead of a space), we would insert commas between the **%f** format commands.

The Assignment Statement

Note that what appears as an equation in expressions is, in fact, an assignment statement and not an algebraic identity. As long as the values of variables on the right of an equals sign are known, the calculated result will be assigned to the variable on the left of the equals sign. As an example, consider the following short program.

```
/* EXAMPLE OF ACCUMULATION */
main( )
{
    float sum;

    sum=0;
    sum=sum+1;
    printf("Accumulated result is %f",sum);
}
```

The third executable statement of the main program would be meaningless had it been an algebraic expression. In computing terms the statement states 'take the present value in **sum**, add one to it and store the result in **sum**'. When this statement is executed, the value of **sum** (set in the previous statement) is zero and adding one to it results in a new value of **sum** equal to one.

Compiling and Executing a Program

The translation of a C program (source file) to a machine specific code (object file) that will eventually be executed by the particular computer is the task of the C compiler. The compiled object file can then be linked to the appropriately selected library routines (supplied with the compiler), and the resulting exec file may or may not be executed immediately; it largely depends on the version of the compiler in your particular machine.

To illustrate the procedure of compiling and executing a C program we shall use here Borland's Turbo C Compiler in an MS-DOS operating environment. The exact steps taken in compiling the source file, linking the resulting object file and then executing the resulting exec file, might vary slightly for different compilers, but the general philosophy remains the same.

It is assumed here that the C compiler has been installed according to the instructions given in the installation manual of your particular package and that appropriate batch and configuration files have been written to allow access to the appropriate sub-directories in which the library and header routines are to be found.

For example, in the case of Turbo C, we assume that the TCC.EXE and TLINK.EXE files of the package have been copied to a sub-directory of the root directory which we shall call \TURBOC.

Further, we assume that all the .LIB and appropriate .OBJ (start-up) files have been copied into a sub-directory called \LIB, while all the .H (header) files have been copied into a sub-directory called \INCLUDE.

To enter the source file for the **average** program, change directory to \TURBOC and use the line editor to create the **average.c** file. Once the source program has been created, we can use the command

    tcc average

which causes the source file of the **average** program to be compiled and linked to the appropriate library routines. The **tcc** command is similar to UNIX's **cc** command.

Note that in this instance, we have not bothered to separate the process of compilation from that of linking; a step that might be desirable under certain circumstances, for example, when linking already compiled subroutines to a newly compiled program.

If compilation is successful, the system creates two files with the following extensions.

    .OBJ   the object file, and
    .EXE   the executable file.

If there are any compilation errors, none of these files will be created. The compiler will simply inform you which line in your source file is in error. In such a case, use your editor to correct the original source file and re-compile. If there are no compilation or linking errors, execution of the program can be started by simply typing the name of the executable file, in this case,

    average

which will cause the computer to respond with

    Enter three numbers:
Typing,

    2 3 5

the three numbers (separated by spaces) corresponding to variables **a**, **b** and **c** in the **scanf** function of the program, causes the computer to respond with

    The average is 3.333333

To re-execute the program, we only need to re-type its name and supply different values to the program variables.

In the case of the UNIX environment, the program is compiled with the command

```
cc average.c
```

and if no errors occur, you'll just get the appropriate *shell* prompt. To execute the compiled program (which is always called **a.out**), type

```
a.out
```

If you want to keep the compiled program, you must rename it before compiling any others by using the **mv** command.

Summary of Some C Rules

- Only the first forty characters of variables and constant names are significant. They should only contain letters, numbers and the underscore, and the first character must be a letter.

- Variable names are customarily written in lower case letters. They must be declared within the **main** program by type and name before they can be used.

- Constant names are customarily written in upper case letters. The must be defined with the **#define** prior to the **main** program and a value must be given to them. The value of a constant must not be changed during execution of the program.

- Integer variables and constants have no decimal point.

- Floating point (also known as real) variables and constants must always have a decimal point.

- The left hand side of an assignment statement must contain only one variable. This variable can be of different type (integer or real) to the expression on the right hand side of the assignment statement. If you mix variable types (also called mixed mode arithmetic), watch out for truncation.

Problems

1.1 Write a program, using the **scanf** function, which assigns three numbers to the variables **days**, **hours** and **minutes** and then calculates and prints the total number of minutes involved. Compile and execute the program.

1.2 Write a program, using the **scanf** function, which can convert degrees Fahrenheit (**f**) to degrees Celsius (**c**). Use the relationship

Degrees Celsius = (Degrees Fahrenheit − 32) * 5/9

Use the **#define** statement to assign the constant 5/9 to FACTOR.

2. OPERATORS & I/O CONTROL

Arithmetic Operators

The symbols *, /, %, +, and − are the standard arithmetic operators in C. With these, together with brackets ( ), to enclose expressions, and the assignments statement (=), allow the manipulation of most arithmetic expressions. For example, the calculations in the **average** program of the previous chapter are performed in the fourth and fifth executable statements of the main program. We can combine these into one statement, by writing

average=(**a**+**b**+**c**)/3.0;   (Not **average**=**a**+**b**+**c**/3.0);

It is important that the numerator of this expression is in brackets. If it were not, C would evaluate first **c**/3.0 and then add to it **a**+**b**, which would give the wrong result. This is due to an in-built system of priorities, as shown below. A full list appears at the end of this chapter.

_____ **Arithmetic Operators and their Priority** _____

C symbol	Example	Priority	Function
( )	(a+b)/c	1	Parenthesized operation
*	a*b	2	Multiplication
/	a/b	2	Division
%	a%b	2	Modulus
+	a+b	3	Addition
−	a−b	3	Subtraction
=	a=b	4	Assignment

On evaluating expressions, C performs arithmetic operations in the order of priority indicated in the table. Expressions in parentheses are evaluated first.

Thus, through the use of parentheses, the order of priority of execution, and therefore the final value of an expression, can be changed. If a line has an expression which contains several operators of equal priority, C will evaluate it from left to right.

Note that in C, the equal (=) sign is a replacement operator. This means that expressions such as

    a = b = c

are permissible, but the order of evaluation is now from right to left, so that **c** would be assigned to **b**, which in turn would be assigned to **a**, giving all three variables the same value, namely that of **c**.

Formatted Output

The **printf** function in C is used to provide a formatted output in a manner similar to that of the FORMAT statement in Fortran. This gives us full control on the layout of the output, as well as the form in which the numbers printed out will appear. The function is implemented as follows:

    printf("format string", variables);

where 'format string' specifies the form in which the variables are to be printed, that is, type of value, spacing, and so on).

To illustrate the mechanism, let us examine a program that calculates a specified percentage of a given value. The listing is given below, and we shall refer to it as the PERCENT program.

```
/* CALCULATE PERCENT */
main( )
{
    float value,rate,percent;

    printf("Enter a number: ");
    scanf("%f",&value);
    printf("Enter % rate: ");
    scanf("%f",&rate);
    percent=value*rate/100;
    printf("Result = %0.2f",percent);
}
```

Note that the last **printf** statement has a 0.2 following the % control character. It specifies that the variable **percent** must be printed out with two digits after the decimal point. The **f** indicates the 'field' type which, in this case, is floating point.

The control characters used to specify field types are shown on the next page.

Type	Meaning
%c	one character output. The prefix **u** (**%uc**) can be used for **unsigned char** type constants.
%d	decimal (base 10), integer values. The prefix **u** or **l** can be used - (**%ud**) for **unsigned int** type number, or (**%ld**) for **long int** type number.
%e	scientific notation (3.6E−5) for expressing very large or very small real numbers.
%f	floating point value - must include a decimal point.
%g	general format to represent values in either e or f format, whichever has the shortest form.
%o	octal (base 8) values.
%p	pointer values.
%s	string variables.
%u	unsigned integers.
%x	hexadecimal (base 16) values.

Examples of using these format controls are given below, with the type of output they will produce shown overleaf.

```
/*FORMAT CONTROLS */
main( )
{
    printf("Single specified character: %c\n",'a');
    printf("ASCII character of decimal 65: %c\n",65);
    printf("Integer 65 in decimal: %d\n", 65);
    printf("Integer with leading zeros: %04d\n",65);
    printf("Scientific notation: %e\n",12345.6);
    printf("Floating point: %0.3f\n",123.45);
    printf("Short general format: %g\n",12.34);
    printf("Short general format: %g\n",0.00000012);
    printf("Octal number 9 in decimal: %o\n",9);
    printf("String variable: %s\n","Hello");
    printf("Hexadecimal of decimal 11: %02x\n",11);

}
```

Note the *escape sequence* (**\n**) within the format string. It simply provides a newline so that the output of the next **printf** statement appears on a separate line.

This, and additional escape sequences which can be used to format output are listed below.

Table of Escape Sequences

Type	Meaning
\\	backslash
\'	single quote
\"	double quote
\?	question mark
\a	audible bell
\b	backspace
\f	formfeed
\n	newline
\0	NULL character
\r	carriage return
\t	tab (horizontal)
\v	vertical tab
\xhhh	insert ASCII code hhh

Note that the **0** (zero) following the **%** control character within the format string of our previous program, forces leading zeros to be printed out. The number following, specifies the width of the printed field.

Type this program into your computer, compile it and run it. On executing the program, the following output should appear on the screen.

```
Single specified character: a
ASCII character of decimal 65: A
Integer 65 in decimal: 65
Integer with leading zeros: 0065
Scientific notation: 1.23456e004
Floating point: 123.450
Short general format: 12.34
Short general format: 1.2e-007
Octal number 9 is decimal: 11
String variable: Hello
Hexadecimal of decimal 11: 0b
```

Character I/O

A string of characters can be entered into a program using the **scanf** function. However, before we give an example, we must mention the fact that when performing character I/O, we need to *include* into our program the **stdio.h** (standard i/o header file). This is done with the **#include** statement which must precede the **main()** program. As was the case with the **#define** statement, the hash sign (**#**) must again be placed in column one of the program. Thus, a program to read in our name could be written as follows:

```
/* USING scanf TO INPUT A STRING */
#include <stdio.h>
main( )
{
    char name[20];

    printf("What is your name? ");
    scanf("%s",name);
    printf("Hello, %s",name);
}
```

Since **name** was declared as an array of 20 characters, the value of **name** is the address of the first character of the array itself. As a result, the address operator (**&**) in front of **name** is not needed.

The above program works correctly, provided you don't include a space in the input string, as would be the case for example if you were typing in your full name, because a space signals the end of a string.

To overcome the above limitation, the **gets** function should be used, which reads in everything you type until you press <Enter>, at which point it appends a null (**\0**) at the end of the input line. This function is used as follows:

```
/* USING gets TO INPUT A STRING */
#include <stdio.h>
main( )
{
    char name[50];

    printf("What is your name? ");
    gets(name);
    printf("Hello, %s",name);
}
```

15

Finally, there is a routine that can accept a single character from the keyboard without echoing it on the screen. This is the **getchar()** function, which takes the following form:

```
letter = getchar( );
```

To output this character, we could use the **putchar()** function, as follows:

```
putchar(letter);
```

which echoes it onto the screen.

The % Operator in Integer Division

Integer division will not give the same results as real number division because integer variables do not contain decimal points. Dividing integer 10 by integer 3 will give the answer 3. The remainder is lost.

The modulus operator (%) gives that remainder. The following program illustrates the point.

```
main( )
{
    int a,b,x=10,y=3;
    a=x/y;
    b=x%y;
    printf("Division result is: %d \n",a);
    printf("Remainder is: %d",b);
}
```

Note the variable declaration and initialization. All four variables are declared integer, while variables **x** and **y** are initialized to 10 and 3, respectively.

On execution, the message

```
Division result is : 3
Remainder is: 1
```

appears on the screen. It must be stressed that the % can only operate on integer operands.

Relational Operators

Relational operators are used within **if** statements known as conditional expressions which will be discussed later. We use relational expressions to determine whether one value is equal to (==) another value. A listing of C's relational operators is shown below.

Table of Relational Operators

C symbol	Example	Meaning
==	a == b	a equal to b
<	a < b	a less than b
<=	a <= b	a less than or equal to b
>	a > b	a greater than b
>=	a >= b	a greater than or equal to b
!=	a != b	a not equal to b

Logical Operators

The power of conditional statements can be increased considerably by combining them with the logical operators AND (&&) and OR (||). For example, we might have the situation where we needed to know whether a number was within the range 0 to 100. With relational statements we would have to test for both

```
if (number > 0)
if (number < 100)
```

whereas a better way would be to include a logical operator and test these within one statement, as shown below:

```
if (number > 0 && number < 100)
```

which states that only if both combinations are met will the value of 1 (the Boolean true) be returned and the block of statements following the test will be executed. If either fails, then the value of 0 (the Boolean false) is returned and none of the block of statements following the test will be executed.

Note that all relational and logical testing is done within brackets and the variable name must be repeated for each relational expression.

The second logical operator can be used in the following way:

```
if (number < 0 || number > 100)
```

which states that when either is true, then the block of statements following the test will be executed. This test will return 0 (the Boolean false) for all numbers between 0 and 100.

Examples of use of both relational and logical operators will be given in Chapter 3, where the control of program flow will be discussed in some detail.

Ternary Operator

C provides a unique type of statement which employs a ternary operator. It can be used as follows:

```
a = (b > c) ? b : c;
```

which has the following effect. If the value in **b** is greater than the value in **c**, then variable **a** takes the value of **b**, else variable **a** takes the value of **c**.

Unary Operators

C has two unique unary operators which do not exist in other high level languages. These are the *increment* operator (++) and the *decrement* operator (--), which add or subtract 1 from an integer variable. To illustrate their use, we write an ACCUMULATION example as follows:

```
/* EXAMPLE OF ACCUMULATION */
main( )
{
    int sum=0;

    sum=sum+1;
    printf("Accumulated result is %d",sum);
}
```

where the declaration and initialization of variable **sum**, which is now an integer, is achieved on one line. We can now rewrite the assignment statement **sum=sum+1;** in the form of an increment operator, as

```
sum=sum++;
```

where the ++ operator increments the value contained in the variable **sum** by 1, and then assigns the result to **sum**.

Similarly, the decrement operator can be used as

```
sum=sum--;
```

to decrement **sum** by 1.

There are four further variations to these operators. These are as follows:

```
sum=a+b++
sum=a+b--
sum=a+ ++b
sum=a+ --b
```

The first means "add **a** and **b** together, assign the result to **sum**, and increment **b** by 1"; the second means "add **a** and **b** together, assign the result to **sum**, and decrement **b** by 1"; the third means "increment **b** by 1, then add the result to **a**, and assign to **sum**"; the fourth means "decrement **b** by 1, then add the result to **a** and assign to **sum**".

Use the following program to verify the previous identities.

```
/* EXAMPLE OF UNARY OPERATORS */
main( )
{
    int sum,a=5,b=3;

    printf("Original values:\n a b\n %d %d\n",a,b);
    sum=a + --b;
    printf("Results are:\n a b sum\n");
    printf("%d %d %d",a,b,sum);
}
```

Try all the above combinations by editing the assignment statement containing the unary operator.

Address Operators

C supports two special address operators: the (&) which returns the *address of* a given variable, which is assigned by the compiler, and the (*) which is the *indirection* operator and returns the character to which the pointer points. The following program will help to illustrate the point.

```
main( )
{
    int number;
    char *salut;

    number=15;
    salut="Sir\n";
    printf("Value= %d Address= %p\n",number, &number);
    printf("Character= %c Address= %p\n",*salut, salut);
}
```

On executing this program, C writes on the screen

```
Value= 15 Address= FFD8
Character= S Address= 009A
```

where the content of **number** is given by Value= 15 followed by its address, and content of ***salut** points to character S (the first letter of 'Sir') followed by its address.

Bitwise Operators

C supports many operations that are normally to be found only in assembler level. Amongst several of these is the ability to apply bitwise operators on variables of type **int** and **char**.

The table below lists the available bitwise operators.

_____ **Table of Bitwise Operators** _____

C symbol	Meaning
&	bitwise AND
|	bitwise OR
^	bitwise exclusive OR
>>	right shift
<<	left shift
~	ones complement

The bitwise AND (&) performs a logical AND for each of the bits in a variable when compared with the bits in a second variable. A bitwise AND (&) operation produces a 1 in each bit location of the result, only if the bits in the same position in both values are 1. Otherwise the result is 0.

For example, if the two variables shown below contain the binary values:

Variable	Binary representation
value_1	10010011
value_2	11110000

then, the operation

   value_1 & value_2

produces   10010000

Similarly, the bitwise OR (|) performs a logical OR on each bit within two variables, resulting with a 1 if either bit in the corresponding locations in the two variables is 1. Thus,

   value_1 | value_2

produces   11110011

if the same binary values for the variables **value_1** and **value_2** are assumed.

A bitwise exclusive OR (^) operation produces 1 in each bit location of the result only if the bits in the same location in either of the variables is 1. Thus,

   value_1 ^ value_2

produces   01100011

The right and left shift operators, shift the bits in a variable to the right or the left, respectively, by a specified number of bits, while the locations being left empty as a result of the shift are filled with zeros. For example, if variable **b_value** contains the binary number 00010011, then

   a_value = b_value << 3

produces the result   10011000.

21

Finally, the ones complement operator (~), has the effect of inverting the bits in each location. Thus, assuming that variable **b_value** contains the binary number 00010011, then the expression

a_value = ~ b_value

will put the binary number 11101100 in variable **a_value**.

Combined Operators

C provides another type of operator which is a short-hand way of assigning the contents of variables. These are:

a *= b;	which is equivalent to	a = a * b;
a /= b;	which is equivalent to	a = a / b;
a += b;	which is equivalent to	a = a + b;
a -= b;	which is equivalent to	a = a - b;
a %= b;	which is equivalent to	a = a % b;
a <<=b;	which is equivalent to	a = a <<b;
a >>=b;	which is equivalent to	a = a >>b;
a &= b;	which is equivalent to	a = a & b;
a |= b;	which is equivalent to	a = a | b;
a ^= b;	which is equivalent to	a = a ^ b;

Although you might never use this form of assignment, you should know of its existence.

Finally, taking into account all the operators available in C, the arithmetic priority is as shown on the next page.

Table of Priority of C Operators

C symbol	Example	Priority	Function
( )	(a+b)/c	1	Parenthesized operation
–	a=–b	2	Unary minus
+	a=+b	2	Unary plus
!	!a	2	Logical NOT
~	a=~b	2	Bitwise complement
&	a=&b	2	Address
*	a=*b	2	Pointer reference
sizeof()	a=sizeof(b)	2	Size of
++	a++ and ++a	2	Increment
––	a–– and ––a	2	Decrement
*	a*b	3	Multiplication
/	a/b	3	Division
%	a%b	3	Modulus
+	a+b	4	Addition
–	a–b	4	Subtraction
>>	a=b>>c	5	Shift right
<<	a=b<<c	5	Shift left
>	a>b	6	Greater than
>=	a>=b	6	Greater or equal
<	a<b	6	Less than
<=	a<=b	6	Less or equal
==	a==b	7	Equal to
!=	a!=b	7	Not equal to
&	a=b&c	7	Bitwise AND
|	a=b|c	8	Bitwise OR
^	a=b^c	9	Bitwise XOR
&&	a&&b	10	Logical AND
||	a||b	11	Logical OR
=	a=b	12	Assignment

Problems

2.1 Write a program to read in a positive floating point number into a variable called **value**, place the integral part of it into variable **integral**, and the fractional part of it into variable **fractional**. Print out the original number, the integral and fractional parts of it, tabulated under appropriate headings.

2.2 Write a program to calculate the cost of electricity at 5.5 pence per unit between quarterly meter readings **low_value** and **hi_value** which represent the 'low meter reading value' and the 'high meter reading value'. The flat quarterly charge, irrespective of units used, is £8.85.

Use the **scanf** function to assign values to **low_value**, **hi_value**, and the **#define** statement to assign the constants to **UNIT_COST** and **FLAT_RATE**.

3. CONTROL OF PROGRAM FLOW

The if Statement
The **if** statement allows conditional program branching which means that we can decide whether to execute certain statements or not. The decision depends on relational tests. In general we can think of the statement as follows:

```
if (relational test is true)
    {
      execute these
      statements
    }
```

To illustrate the point, refer to the program below which asks you to enter a number. If that number is in the range 5-10, the program prints the message

```
True
```

otherwise it ends without any message appearing on the screen. Note the absence of semicolon at the end of **if**.

```
/* CHECK FOR SPECIFIED RANGE */
main ( )
{
    int number;

    printf("Enter a number (5-10 true)\n");
    scanf("%d",&number);
    if (number>=5 && number<=10)
      printf("True \n");
}
```

An alternative program, to check whether the number is outside a specified range, would be

```
main ( )
{
    int number;

    printf("Enter a number (5-10 not true)\n");
    scanf("%d",&number);
    if (number<5 || number>10)
      printf("True \n");
}
```

The if..else Statement

In many cases we have to perform an **if** statement twice over to detect which of two similar conditions is true, as illustrated below.

```
/* THE TWO if STATEMENTS */
main( )
{
    int number;

    printf("Enter a number between 1 and 99: ");
    scanf("%d",number);
    if (number < 10)
     printf("One digit number");
    if (number > 9)
     printf("two digit number");
}
```

A more advanced version of the **if** statement allows both actions to be inserted in its trailer. The statement takes the following form:

```
if (relational test is true)
    {
     execute these
     statements
    }
else
    {
     execute these
     statements
    }
```

An example of this is incorporated in the modified program below.

```
/* USE OF THE if..else STATEMENTS */
main( )
{
    int number;

    printf("Enter a number between 1 and 99: ");
    scanf("%d",&number);
    if (number < 10)
     printf("One digit number");
    else
     printf("two digit number");
}
```

Note that braces under the **if** or **else** statements are only required if statements following them occupy more than one line. Execute the program and supply numbers between 1 and 99. Obviously, if you type in numbers greater than 99 the program will not function correctly in its present form. But assuming that you have obeyed the message and typed 50 the **printf** statement after the **else** will be executed. On the other hand, if the number typed is less than 10, the first **printf** statement will be executed.

Nested if..else Statements

The above program can be made to test for the correct input range by the inclusion of the AND (**&&**) logical operator within an additional **if..else** statement, as follows:

```
/* USE OF THE if..else AND && STATEMENTS */
main( )
{
    int number;

    printf("Enter a number between 1 and 99: ");
    scanf("%d",&number);
    if (number > 0 && number < 100)
      {
        if (number < 10)
          printf("One digit number");
        else
          printf("two digit number");
      }
    else
        printf("Number not within range");
}
```

Type in the additions to the program, compile and execute it.

The while Loop

The **while** loop provides a mechanism for repeating a group of C statements. The general form of the statement is:

```
while (condition)
    {
      execute these
      statements
}
```

27

We can modify the previous program to incorporate the **while** loop so that the program is repeated provided it is supplied with a positive number. When a number less than 1 is typed in response to the message "Enter a number between 1 and 99: ", the program stops.

```
/* USE OF THE while LOOP */
main( )
{
    int number=1;

    while (number > 0)
     {
        printf("Enter a number between 1 and 99: ");
        scanf("%d",&number);
        if (number > 0 && number < 100)
          {
            if (number < 10)
              printf("One digit number \n");
            else
              printf("two digit number \n");
          }
        else
          printf("Number not within range \n");
     }
}
```

Note the initialization of the integer variable **number** - this is only required in this particular program because of the logic incorporated in the design of the program itself, and is not a necessary part of the **while** loop. Also, note the inclusion of the line feed character (**\n**) in some of the **printf** statements which help in the presentation of information on the screen.

The do while Loop

The **do while** loop is similar to the "repeat until" loop of other high-level languages. It allows the execution of certain instructions at least once, and then tests to find out whether the group of instructions should be repeated. The following program illustrates the method.

```
/* THE do while LOOP */
#include <stdio.h>
main( )
{
    char letter;

    printf("Press Y or N only\n");
    do
     {
      letter=getchar();
     }
    while (letter != 'Y' && letter != 'N');
    printf("You pressed ");
    putchar(letter);
}
```

On executing this program, the command **getchar( )** will be repeated until **letter** holds the value Y or N. Note that the specified letters must be in upper case.

To avoid having to type a letter in a specific case, use either the **toupper( )** or the **tolower( )** command, immediately below the **getchar( )** command, as follows:

    letter=toupper(letter);

or by replacing both these lines by the statement

    letter=toupper(getchar( ));

Although a single instruction is employed between the **do** and **while** elements of the loop in the above example, it has been enclosed in braces to illustrate their place in case of compounded instructions.

The for Loop
The **for** statement marks the beginning code which will be executed repeatedly according to the conditions supplied by the *control* variable within the **for** loop. The general form of the statement is

    for (initialization; condition; increment)

with the 'initialization' and 'increment' portions of the statement being optional. The statement can be either a single instruction or a collection of code enclosed in braces.

To illustrate the point, a simple example is given below.

```
/* EXAMPLE USING THE for LOOP */
main( )
{
    int k;

    for (k=1; k<=5; k++)
    printf("%d\n",k);
}
```

In the **for** statement, the control variable **k** is assigned the value 1 which is increased repeatedly by the last portion of the statement until it reaches 5 (the condition in the middle of the three portions of the statement). It thus has the values 1, 2, 3, 4 and 5. Since it cannot have these values simultaneously, a loop is formed beginning with the **for** statement and ending with the semicolon of the statement below it.

The statements within the loop are re-executed five times, each time with a new value for **k**, until such time as the value of the control variable **k** exceeds its final assigned value of 5. When this happens, program control passes to whatever statement follows the semicolon (in the case of a single statement) or the closing brace (in the case of compounded statements).

The control variable within a **for** loop can be assigned integer, real or double precision values, provided the control variable name has been declared appropriately. In addition, in the case of a real control variable, the increment could be less than unity. The following program converts the values 1, 1.5, 2.0, 2.5, etc, inches, into centimetres.

```
/* CONVERTING INCHES TO CENTIMETRES */
main( )
{
    float inches,centims;

    printf("Inches\t Centimetres\n");
    for (inches=1; inches<=5; inches+=0.5)
      {
        centims=2.54*inches;
        printf("%6.2f %7.2f\n",inches, centims);
      }
}
```

The output should be as follows:

Inches	Centimetres
1.00	2.54
1.50	3.81
2.00	5.08
2.50	6.35
3.00	7.62
3.50	8.89
4.00	10.16
4.50	11.43
5.00	12.70

A negative increment is legal in C. For example

```
main( )
{
    int x;

    for (x=5; x>=1; x--)
      printf("%d\n",x);
}
```

will print the values 5, 4, 3, 2 and 1.

Finally, the initialization and increment portions of a **for** loop are not limited to one variable. It is possible, for example, to initialize two variables, and continue to increment the first and decrement the second for as long as they are not equal. The following example helps to illustrate the point.

```
/* INITIALIZING AND INCREMENTING TWO */
/* CONTROL VARIABLES WITHIN A for LOOP */
main( )
{
    int x,y;

    printf(" X\t Y\n");
    for (x=15, y=-5; x!=y; x--,y++)
    printf("%d %8d\n",x,y);
}
```

Here, **x** is initialized to 15 and decremented by one, while **y** is initialized to –5 and incremented by one. This will continue for as long as the condition **x != y** (**x** not equal to **y**) is met. the last printout will occur when **x** is equal to 6 and **y** is equal to 4.

Nested Loops

Iterative constructs can be nested to allow programming of loops within loops as shown in the example below.

```
/* NESTED for LOOPS */
main( )
{
    int i,j;

    for (i=1; i<=2; i++)
    {
    printf("Outer loop with i= %d\n", i);
    for (j=1; j<=3; j++)
    {
        printf("\t Inner loop with j= %d\n", j);
    }
    }
}
```

On execution, two loops are set up as follows:

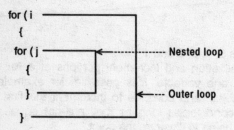

The outer loop is initialized with **i=1** and immediately the inner nested loop is executed 3 times. Then, variable **i** is incremented by 1, so that now **i=2** and the nested loop is executed another 3 times. The output is as follows:

```
Outer loop with i = 1
            Inner loop with j = 1
            Inner loop with j = 2
            Inner loop with j = 3
Outer loop with i = 2
            Inner loop with j = 1
            Inner loop with j = 2
            Inner loop with j = 3
```

Additional levels of nesting are possible. However, deep nesting is costly in terms of memory space.

Speeding up Loops by Using Registers

Amongst the low-level operations that C allows is the direct placement by the compiler of specified variables in registers. This provides significant improvement in speed of access over the slower process of continually referencing main memory for the values of such variables. To utilise this feature, the compiler must be informed of our intention with the use of the **register** command within the declaration statement.

For example, the previous program can be rewritten as follows:

```
/* USING THE register COMMAND */
/* TO SPEEDUP VARIABLE ACCESS */
main( )
{
    register int x,y;

    printf(" X\t Y\n");
    for (x=15, y=-5; x!=y; x--,y++)
      printf("%d %8d\n",x,y);
}
```

The program is identical but for the inclusion of the **register** command in the declaration statement.

Unconditional Program Branching

C provides three statements which cause unconditional program branching. These are: the **goto**, the **continue** and the **break** statements.

Of these, the **goto** statement should be avoided as much as possible, as its use tends to result in 'unstructured' code which can lead to programming errors. The use of the **continue** statement should be severely restricted, as it is possible to write code to carry out the same program flow in a more efficient way. Finally, the **break** statement should only be used with the **switch** command.

The goto Statement:

The **goto** statement provides unconditional program branching; it causes an immediate jump to an indicated statement label. Program execution continues sequentially again, beginning with the line just reached. The general form of the statement can be illustrated as follows:

```
start: if (condition) goto done;

        block of statements
        to be executed if
        (condition) is not true

        goto start;
done:
```

In the above program the first **goto** statement can send program execution to label **done:**, while the second sends program execution back to label **start:**.

The continue Statement:

The **continue** statement causes the immediate execution of the next iteration of a loop and as such, it alters the flow of control within a loop. The following program, which prints out the even numbers between 1 and 40, will help to illustrate the point.

```
/* ILLUSTRATING THE continue STATEMENT */
main( )
{
    int number;
    for (number=1; number<40; number++)
      {
      if ((number % 2) == 0) continue;
        printf("%d \n", number);
      }
}
```

On executing the program, only the odd numbers are printed out because, if the variable **number** holds an even value, the remainder of the integer division is equal to zero, therefore the **continue** portion of the **if** statement is executed, which causes the immediate execution of the next iteration of the loop.

The break Statement:

The **break** statement also affects the control of program flow within a loop, by allowing the program to exit the loop. The statement is mostly used in the **switch** command which will be discussed next.

In the case of nested loops, the **break** statement causes the execution of the nested (currently executing) loop to cease, while the outer loop continues executing.

34

An interesting use of the **for** with the **break** statement can be used in setting up repeatedly accessible menus. For example,

```
for (;;)  /* sets up an infinite loop */
{
    printf("Press a key: ");
    ch=getchar( );
    if (ch=='q')
      break;
}
```

will set up an infinite loop which can only be broken out of by pressing the character q.

The switch Command

The **switch** command is one of C's aids to writing readable programs and provides an efficient alternative to multiple **if** statements. For example, assume we had the code

```
if day=='S'
    printf("Weekend ");
else if day=='M'
    printf("Week day");
else if day=='T'
    printf("Week day");
else if day=='W'
    printf("Week day");
else if day=='F'
    printf("Week day");
else
    printf("Not a day");
```

A more efficient way of writing this code would be the adoption the **switch** command in the following way.

```
/* USING THE switch COMMAND */
#include <stdio.h>

main( )
{
    char day;

    printf("Which day? ");
    day=getchar();

    switch(day) {
     case 'S': printf("Weekend "); break;
     case 'M': printf("Week day"); break;
     case 'T': printf("Week day"); break;
     case 'W': printf("Week day"); break;
     case 'F': printf("Week day"); break;
     default: printf("Not a day");
    }
}
```

Typing the first letter of a named day, displays whether that day is part of the weekend or a week day. Any other character causes the program to display the **default** value.

Problems

3.1 Write a program that reads in the examination number of candidates (in the range 0-32768), together with the percentage marks attained in a given examination. The marks have to be graded as follows:

Over 70%, A; 60-69%, B; 50-59%, C; 40-49%, D; Below 40%, F.

The program should print, under suitable headings, the candidate number, mark and grade for each candidate. Arrange for the program to stop when a negative candidate number is entered.

3.2 Compound interest can be calculated using the formula

$A = P * (1+R/100)^n$

where P is the original money lent, A is what it amounts to in n years at R per cent per annum interest.

Write a program to calculate the amount of money owed after n years, where n changes from 1 to 15 in yearly increments, if the money lent originally is £5,000 and the interest rate remains constant throughout this period at 11.5%. Format the output to restrict calculated values to two decimal places and tabulate the results.

4. ARRAYS & POINTERS

Defining a String

Just as numerical values can be assigned to variables and constants, strings can be assigned to character variables, provided they have been declared in a **char** statement. Even though C does not support a separate string data type, it allows for two different methods for defining strings. One method is to use a *character array*, while the other is to use a *character pointer*. Both techniques have been used previously in this book, while discussing various types of C operators, but now the subject will be discussed to some depth.

Character Array Definition:

As an example of character array definition, we will use the following program.

```
/* USING A CHARACTER ARRAY */
/* TO DEFINE A STRING */
main( )
{
    char name[15];

    strcpy(name,"Mr Goodfellow");
    puts(name);
}
```

The [15] after the variable **name** instructs the compiler to set aside an array of 14 **char** variables, with the 15th space being taken by the *null character* \0. On executing the **strcpy** statement, the compiler creates the string "Mr Goodfellow", followed by the null character \0. It then calls a function called **strcpy**, which copies the string, character by character, into the memory location pointed to by **name**, until it copies the null character. When the **puts(name)** function is executed, the compiler passes the address in **name** which points to the first letter of the string in memory and then checks for a null character at that address; if it finds one it ceases operation, otherwise it prints the character, adds one to the address and checks the character in the new location for a null.

As a result of this dependency on a null character terminator, C can have strings of any length, provided there is sufficient memory to hold them.

The following program will help to explain how the **strcpy** function works. The program uses the **getchar()** function within a **for** loop to get each character from the keyboard. When all the expected characters have been fetched, then a null (**\0**) character is appended to the string.

```
/* USING A CHARACTER ARRAY */
/* TO DEFINE A STRING */
#include <stdio.h>
main( )
{
    int count;
    char name[10];

    printf("Type 'Goodfellow'\n\n");
    for (count=0; count<10; count++)
      name[count]=getchar();
    name[count]='\0';
    printf("\nHello, Mr ");
    puts(name);
}
```

Similarly, the following program could be used to display the characters held in array **name**, one at a time, with the use of the **putchar()** function within a **for** loop.

```
/* USING CHARACTER ARRAY */
/* TO DEFINE A STRING */
#include <stdio.h>
main( )
{
    int count;
    char name[15];

    strcpy(name,"Mr Goodfellow");
    printf("Hello, ");
    for (count=0; name[count] != '\0'; count++)
      putchar(name[count]);
}
```

The above program shows how, by incorporating the null (**\0**) character at the end of a string, we can read the contents of a string array without having to know its actual length.

Character Pointer Definition:

The second definition of a string can be achieved through a *character pointer*. To illustrate this, edit as follows, the first program used to show how a character array can be used to define a string.

```
/* USING A CHARACTER POINTER */
/* TO DEFINE A STRING */
main( )
{
    char *name;

    name="Mr Goodfellow";
    printf("Hello, ");
    puts(name);
}
```

The * in front of **name** tells the compiler that **name** is a pointer which holds the address of the first character of a string. The asterisk (*) is known as the indirection operator and returns the character to which the pointer points. When the compiler executes the program and comes across the statement **name="Mr Goodfellow"**;, it creates the string "Mr Goodfellow", followed by a null (\0) character somewhere within the object code file, and then assigns the starting address of that string to **variable name**.

Pointer Memory Allocation

When a variable is declared as **int** or **float** and a string is declared in **char** as an array of characters, memory space for that variable or string is automatically allocated. However, when a variable is declared as a pointer to **int** or **float**, and a string is declared as a pointer to **char**, no specific space in memory is allocated to store these variables; the pointer simply refers to any random location in memory and, since other declarations will allocate the same area of memory, the space used for such objects may become corrupted.

To overcome the above problem, such pointers must be initialised to point to a currently allocated area of the program heap. To do this, the pointer is assigned the value returned from the **malloc** family of functions.

The function, in the case of a string, is used as follows:

```
/* USING malloc TO ALLOCATE MEMORY */
/* TO A CHARACTER POINTER */
#include <alloc.h>
main( )
{
    char *name;

    name=(char *) malloc(14);
    strcpy(name,"Mr Goodfellow");
    printf("Hello, ");
    puts(name);
}
```

The call to **malloc** sets aside 14 bytes (one extra for the end of string marker) of memory and assigns the address of that memory to **name.**

Similarly, in the case of variable numbers, the function is used as follows:

```
/* USING malloc TO ALLOCATE MEMORY */
/* TO A VARIABLE POINTER */
#include <alloc.h>
main( )
{
    int *number;

    number=(int *) malloc(sizeof(int));
    *number=555;
    printf("Address of no.: %p\n", number);
    printf("Value of no.:  %d", *number);
}
```

The statement **number=(int *) malloc(sizeof(int));** has the following effect: First, the **sizeof(int)** returns the number of bytes required to store a variable of type **int**; then, **malloc( )** allocates that number of consecutive bytes of the available memory to store the number; then, it returns the starting address of those bytes. The **(int *)** part of the statement, type casts the pointer as type **int**.

On executing this program, it writes

```
Address of number: 03EC
Value of number: 555
```

on the display.

String Arrays

A number of strings can be stored under a common name in what is known as a string array. Let us assume that we have four names i.e. SMITH, JONES, BROWN and WILSON which we would like to store in a string array. The following program will achieve this.

```
/* USING STRING ARRAYS */
main( )
{
    int i;
    char names[4][6];

    strcpy(names[0],"SMITH");
    strcpy(names[1],"JONES");
    strcpy(names[2],"BROWN");
    strcpy(names[3],"WILSON");
    for (i=0; i<4; i++)
      puts(names[i]);
}
```

Alternatively, we could use an array of pointers to do the same job, as follows:

```
/* USING ARRAYS OF POINTERS */
#include <alloc.h>
main( )
{
    int i;
    char *names[4];

    for (i=0; i<4; i++)
      names[i]=(char *) malloc(6);
    names[0]="SMITH";
    names[1]="JONES";
    names[2]="BROWN";
    names[3]="WILSON";
    for (i=0; i<4; i++)
      puts(names[i]);
}
```

The definition **char *names[4];**, informs the compiler that we intend to use an array of pointers to character strings.

Using arrays of pointers, rather than string arrays, allows for easy manipulation of strings.

For example, to swap two strings around, it merely requires the swapping of the pointers, as opposed to having to exchange each string, character by character. The following program, which sorts a number of strings in alphabetical order, will help to illustrate the technique.

```
/* SORTING A LIST OF STRINGS */
#include <alloc.h>
#include <string.h>
main( )
{
    int i,j,k;
    char *names[4], *temp;

    for (i=0; i<4; i++)
      names[i]=(char *) malloc(6);
    temp=(char *) malloc(6);
    names[0]="SMITH";
    names[1]="JONES";
    names[2]="BROWN";
    names[3]="WILSON";

    printf("Unsorted list\n");
    for (i=0; i<4; i++)
      puts(names[i]);

    for (i=0; i<3; i++)                    \* Start of sort routine *\
      {
      for (j=0; j<3; j++)
       if (strcmp(names[j], names[j+1]) > 0)
        {
          temp=names[j];
          names[j]=names[j+1];
          names[j+1]=temp;
        }
      printf("\nSorted list %d\n",i);
      for (k=0; k<4; k++)
        puts(names[k]);
      }                                    \* End of sort routine *\
}
```

The 'start' and 'end' of the sort routine are marked with comment lines. Note the use of the C function **strcmp** which requires the header file **string.h** to be 'included'.

The **strcmp** function compares two strings, character by character, according to the ASCII conversion codes (see table below) and returns a value (<0, 0, >0) based on the results of comparing **str1** (or part of it) to **str2** (or part of it).

On compiling and executing the program you will see that information appears on the screen in such a manner as to allow us to distinguish the result of each execution of the outer **for** loop (by printing the list of strings in the order they happen to be at the time). What you see on the screen is:

```
Unsorted list
SMITH
JONES
BROWN
WILSON

Sorted list 0
JONES
BROWN
SMITH
WILSON

Sorted list 1
BROWN
JONES
SMITH
WILSON

Sorted list 2
BROWN
JONES
SMITH
WILSON
```

Within the nested **for** loop, when j=0, the first string of the list is compared with the second and if it is found to be larger, the two strings are interchanged using **temp** as a temporary string for the swap. When j=1, the second string is compared with the third, and so on until j=3, when the penultimate string is compared with the last.

This process is repeated (with the use of the outer **for** loop) n–1 times, where n is the total number of strings in the list. Obviously, there is room for improvement here, because if the list of strings were in order, we still force the nested **for** loop to be repeated n–1 times.

Table of ASCII Conversion Codes

CHAR	ABBR	DEC	CHAR	ABBR	DEC	CHAR	ABBR	DEC
CTRL @	nul	0	CTRL K	vt	11	CTRL V	syn	22
CTRL A	soh	1	CTRL L	ff	12	CTRL W	etb	23
CTRL B	stx	2	CTRL M	cr	13	CTRL X	can	24
CTRL C	etx	3	CTRL N	so	14	CTRL Y	em	25
CTRL D	eot	4	CTRL O	si	15	CTRL Z	sub	26
CTRL E	enq	5	CTRL P	dle	16	CTRL [	esc	27
CTRL F	ack	6	CTRL Q	dc1	17	CTRL \	fs	28
CTRL G	bel	7	CTRL R	dc2	18	CTRL]	gs	29
CTRL H	bs	8	CTRL S	dc3	19	CTRL ^	rs	30
CTRL I	ht	9	CTRL T	dc4	20	CTRL _	us	31
CTRL J	lf	10	CTRL U	nak	21			

CHAR	DEC	CHAR	DEC	CHAR	DEC
SPACE	32	@	64	'	96
!	33	A	65	a	97
"	34	B	66	b	98
#	35	C	67	c	99
$	36	D	68	d	100
%	37	E	69	e	101
&	38	F	70	f	102
'	39	G	71	g	103
(	40	H	72	h	104
)	41	I	73	i	105
*	42	J	74	j	106
+	43	K	75	k	107
,	44	L	76	l	108
-	45	M	77	m	109
.	46	N	78	n	110
/	47	O	79	o	111
0	48	P	80	p	112
1	49	Q	81	q	113
2	50	R	82	r	114
3	51	S	83	s	115
4	52	T	84	t	116
5	53	U	85	u	117
6	54	V	86	v	118
7	55	W	87	w	119
8	56	X	88	x	120
9	57	Y	89	y	121
:	58	Z	90	z	122
;	59	[	91	{	123
<	60	\	92			124
=	61	]	93	}	125
>	62	^	94	~	126
?	63	_	95	del	127

Note: In the above table, groups of two or three lower case letters are abbreviations for standard ASCII control characters. Codes within the range 128 to 255 form the extended IBM character set. This can be accessed by typing a number within the range 128 to 255 on the numeric key pad while holding down the 'Alt' key. On releasing the Alt key the character represented by the typed decimal will appear on the screen.

String and Substring Manipulation

We shall now introduce a method which allows substring manipulation. For example, suppose we want to sort our previous list of strings to a depth of **n** characters only, so that names like Smith and Smyth were not actually sorted, if we chose a sort depth of two characters. We can achieve this by the simple replacement of the 'string comparison' statement in the 'Sorting a List of Strings' program, by

```
strncmp (names[j], names[j+1], number)
```

where **number** is the number of characters to be considered in our logical comparisons. Note that the function name **strncmp** now includes the letter **n**, as its purpose, and effect, is different from that of the **strcmp** function.

A list of the 25 string functions available in C, is given in the table at the end of this chapter.

Perhaps the most important use of string manipulation is that of building up string overlays. What we mean by this is the ability to create an empty string of fixed length, and then place characters in it anywhere along its length. The following program will help to illustrate this effect. Note the allocation of characters into the three strings **line**, **aster** and **blank**, as shown below:

```
line="                                        ";
aster="*";
blank="";
```

particularly string **line** which has forty spaces between the two quotes. Also note the functions within the **puts** statement, which is reproduced below.

```
puts(strcat(strncat(blank,line,pos-1),aster));
```

The two function calls within the **puts** statement can be simplified by considering the innermost function first, which is

```
strncat(blank,line,pos-1);
```

and states 'string concatenate n characters (in this case, **pos-1**) from the second string (**line**) to the first string (**blank**). The 'result' of this operation is then used by the outer function, namely,

```
strcat(result,aster);
```

where **result** is what the innermost function returned. The **strcat** function simply concatenates **aster** to **result**. The full program listing is given below.

```
/* OVERLAY OF STRINGS */
#include <alloc.h>
#include <string.h>
#define MAX_LEN 40
main( )
{
    int pos;
    char *line, *aster, *blank;

    line=(char *) malloc(MAX_LEN);
    aster=(char *) malloc(1);
    blank=(char *) malloc(1);
    line="                    ";
    aster="*";
    blank="";

    printf("Enter position of star (1-40): ");
    scanf("%d",&pos);

    if (pos > 0 && pos < 41)
      {
      printf("\n");
      printf("          1         2         3         4\n");
      printf ("1234567890123456789012345678901234567890\n");
      puts(strcat(strncat(blank,line,pos-1),aster));
      }
    else
      printf("Out of range");
}
```

In the **char** declaration we inform the compiler of three pointers to strings **line**, **aster** and **blank**, the contents of which were discussed earlier. We then input the position we would like to see an asterisk in our output into **int** variable **pos**. Subsequently, we concatenate **pos-1** spaces to the end of **blank** which is one blank character in length (thus, the **pos-1** blank character selected form **line**). To this, we then concatenate a single asterisk and print out the final result under a 'line ruler' so that we can check the exact position of the asterisk.

This overlay technique could be used to present visually the results of an experiment in the form of a scatter plot or a crude graph, although the reason for introducing the technique here was to introduce several string functions.

Subscripted Numerical Variables

Subscripted numerical variables permit the representation of many quantities with one variable name. A particular quantity is indicated by writing a subscript in square brackets after the variable name. Individual quantities are called elements, while a set of elements is called an array. A subscripted numerical variable may have one, two or three subscripts and it then represents a one-, two- or three-dimensional numerical array.

The elements of a one-dimensional array can be represented as follows:

A[0]   A[1]   A[2]   A[3]

while those of a two-dimensional array as:

A[0][0]   A[0][1]   A[0][2]   A[0][3]
A[1][0]   A[1][1]   A[1][2]   A[1][3]
A[2][0]   A[2][1]   A[2][2]   A[2][3]

The first of the two subscripts refers to the row number, starting at 0, while the second subscript refers to the column number, again starting from 0. Thus, the above array is a 3 row by 4 column table.

A three-dimensional array can be thought of as stacked two-dimensional arrays with the third subscript, running from 0 to the maximum height of the stack, thus forming a cube, while a four-dimensional array will be a row of cubes, and so on.

In the computer, however, arrays are stored with elements following one another on a single line as shown below.

A[0][0]   A[1][0]   A[2][0]   A[0][1]   A[1][1]   A[2][1]

with the first subscript changing more rapidly than the second, and the second more rapidly than the third (in the case of a three-dimensional array). Provided that this is recognized and understood, we can use the previously discussed tabular form of representation for programming purposes.

Arrays must be declared in a declaration statement such as

type name[rows][columns][height]...[sizeN]

which must precede any executable statements in a program.

The following program illustrates the use of numerical arrays. Data are read into a one-dimensional array and subsequently the contents of the even numbered elements are summed into variable **even**, while the contents of all the odd elements are summed into variable **odd**.

```
/* SUMMING ELEMENTS OF AN ARRAY */
#include <stdio.h>
#define COL 16

main( )
{
    int value[COL];
    int i, even=0, odd=0;

    printf("Enter the following %d numbers\n\n",COL);
    printf("7,6,1,9,7,14,39,24,19,32,21,8,5,15,28,4");
    printf("\n\n");
    for (i=0; i<COL; i++)
     {
     printf("No. %d\t ",i+1);
     scanf("%d",&value[i]);
     }
    for (i=0; i<COL; i+=2)          /* SUM EVEN ELEMENTS */
      even+=value[i];
    for (i=1; i<COL; i+=2)          /* SUM ODD ELEMENTS  */
      odd+=value[i];
    printf("\nSum of even elements = %d",even);
    printf("\nSum of odd elements  = %d",odd);

}
```

On executing this program, and entering the 16 suggested numbers, the output

```
Sum of even elements = 127
Sum of odd elements  = 112
```

is printed on the screen.

The Bubble Sort Technique

The following program illustrates the use of numerical arrays as implemented within the bubble sort technique.

```c
/* BUBBLE SORT TECHNIQUE */
#include <stdio.h>
#define COL 16

main( )
{
    int value[COL];
    int i,j,temp,max,flag;

    printf("Enter the following %d numbers\n\n",COL);
    printf("7,6,1,9,7,14,39,24,19,32,21,8,5,15,28,4\n");
    printf("\nUnsorted list\n");
    for (i=0; i<COL; i++)
     scanf("%d",&value[i]);
    max=COL;
    for (i=0; i<COL-1; i++)
     {
     max=max-1;
     flag=0;
     for (j=0; j<max; j++)
      if (value[j] > value[j+1])
       {
         temp=value[j];
         value[j]=value[j+1];
         value[j+1]=temp;
         flag=1;
       }
     if (flag == 0) break;
     }
    printf("\nSorted list\n");
    for (i=0; i<COL; i++)
     printf("%d ",value[i]);
}
```

The numbers to be sorted are best entered with spaces between them, so that they can appear on one line, making it easier to check against the suggested input. The output of the program then appears, sorted in ascending order, on the line below.

Since the highest valued number drops to the bottom of the list, we can reduce the upper limit (represented by variable **max**) of the **j** (inner) loop by one for each execution of the **i** (outer) loop, thus reducing the total number of comparisons to a minimum. Also, while the full **COL-1** iterations may be needed in the worst case, the list will often be sorted in somewhere between **0** and **COL-1** iterations. This can be overcome by incorporating a **flag** in the program whose value is set to 0 normally, but is reset to 1 every time an exchange takes place. By testing for the value of the **flag** at the end of each iteration of the inner loop, we can tell whether or not we need to execute the outer loop one more time. Type the program into your computer, save it under the filename **bubble**, compile and execute it.

_____Table of String Functions_____

Function Call	Operation
strcat(str1,str2)	Concatenates (appends) string str2 to str1
strncat(str1,str2,n)	Concatenates n number f bytes from string str2 to str1
strcmp(str1,str2)	Compares string str2 to str1. Returns a value (<0, 0 or >0) based on result of comparison
stricmp(str1,str2)	Compares string str2 to str1, without case sensitivity
strnicmp(str1,str2,n)	Compares n number of bytes from string str2 to str1, without case sensitivity
strcpy(str1,str2)	Copies string str2 into str1

strdup(pnt,strn)	Copies a string into a new location, returning a pointer
strncpy(str1,str2,n)	Copies n number of bytes from str2 to str1
strlwr(strn)	Converts upper case letters in a string to lower case
strupr(strn)	Converts lower case letters in a string to upper case
strlen(strn)	Returns the length of a string
strrev(strn)	Reverses a string and returns a pointer
strtod(strn)	Converts a string to a **double** value
strtol(strn)	Converts a string to a **long** value
strchr(strn,chr)	Scans string strn for the first occurrence of a character in chr, returning a pointer
strcspn(str1,str2)	Scans string str1 for the first segment not containing any subset of characters in str2, and returns a pointer
strpbrk(str1,str2)	Scans string str1 for the first occurrence of any character from string str2
strrchr(strn,chr)	Scans a string (in the reverse direction) for the last occurrence of a given character
strspn(str1,str2)	Scans string str1 for the first segment that is a subset of str2, returning its length
strstr(str1,str2)	Scans string str2 for occurrence of string str1, returning a pointer to the element in str2

strtok(str1,str2)	Scans string str1 for delimited tokens which are defined in string str2
strnset(strn,n,chr)	Sets n number of bytes in string strn to a given character in chr
strset(strn,chr)	Sets all characters in string strn to a given character in chr

---

Problems

4.1 Modify the 'String Sorting' program, to be found under the 'String Arrays' section of this chapter, so that it is written in general form and can accept a specified number of **names** (of specified length) from the keyboard, before sorting them in alphabetical order. Use the **#define** statement to define MAX_NUM (the maximum number of strings) and MAX_LEN (their length) as constants.

4.2 The Fibonacci sequence starts with the numbers 1 and 1. The next number is the sum of these and subsequent numbers are the sum of the preceding pair. So we get:

1, 1, 2, 3, 5, 8, 13, 21, ...

Write a program to calculate the first 12 Fibonacci numbers and store them in an integer one-dimensional array **series**, while in a second one-dimensional array **sum**, store the average of adjacent numbers. Note that array **sum** must be capable of storing floating point numbers, if the result of averaging is to be correct.

Arrange for the printout to be headed appropriately.

5. FUNCTIONS

Standard Arithmetic Functions

C contains standard functions to perform many mathematical operations. They relieve the user from programming his own small routines to calculate such common functions as sines of angles, square roots, logarithms, and so on. Standard mathematical functions have a call name followed by a parenthesized argument. They are pre-defined (requiring the **stdlib.h** or **math.h** header files), and as such may be used anywhere in a program. C's most common standard functions are listed below.

_____Standard C Functions_____

Call Name	Meaning	Type
abs(n)	Absolute value of n	int
acos(x)	Arc-cosine of x	double
asin(x)	Arc-sine of x	double
atan(x)	Arc-tangent of x	double
atof(ch)	Converts string to number	double
atoi(ch)	Converts string to integer	int
atol(ch)	Converts string to long	long
cos(x)	Cosine of angle x	double
cosh(x)	Hyperbolic cosine of x	double
ecvt(x)	Converts number to string	double
exp(x)	Raises e to the power of x	double
fabs(x)	Absolute value of x	double
fmod(x,y)	Calculates remainder of x/y	double
hypot(x,y)	Calculates hypotenuse	double
labs(x)	Absolute value of x	long
log(x)	Natural logarithm of x	double
log10(x)	Logarithm to base 10 of x	double
poly(x,n,c[])	Generates nth polynomial in x	double
pow(x,y)	Raises x to power of y	double
pow10(n)	Raises 10 to power of n	int
rand(void)	Random number generator	int
sin(x)	Sine of angle x	double
sinh(x)	Hyperbolic sine	double
sqrt(x)	Returns the square root of x	double
tan(x)	Tangent of angle X	double
tanh(x)	Hyperbolic tangent	double

Function calls can be used as expressions or elements of expressions wherever expressions are legal. A further explanation of the use of these functions is given below.

sin(x), cos(x) and tan(x):
The sine, cosine and tangent functions require an argument angle expressed in radians. If the angle is stated in degrees, conversion to radians can be achieved with the relation Radians=Degrees*PI/180.0, where PI=3.141592654.

asin(x), acos(x) and atan(x):
The arc-sine, arc-cosine and arc-tangent functions return a value in radians, in the range +1.570796 to –1.570796 corresponding to the value of a sine, cosine or tangent supplied as the argument **x**. Conversion to degrees is achieved with the relation Degrees=Radians*180.0/PI, where PI=3.141592654.

hypot(x,y):
The **hypot( )** function calculates the hypotenuse of a right-angle triangle of sides **x** and **y**.

sqrt(x):
The **sqrt( )** function returns the square root of the number supplied to it.

We shall illustrate the use of the above functions by considering a simple problem involving a 2 m long ladder resting against a wall. We assume that the angle between ladder and ground is 60 degrees and with the help of simple trigonometry we shall work out the vertical distance between the top of the ladder and the ground, the horizontal distance between the foot of the ladder and the wall and also the ratio of the vertical to horizontal distance.

The program on the next page uses the trigonometric functions **sin( )**, **cos( )**, **tan( )**, **atan( )** and also the function **hypot( )** to solve the problem. In addition, it calculates the original angle and ladder length.

```
/* LADDER AGAINST WALL */
#include <math.h>
#define PI 3.141592654

main( )
{
    double angle,length,arads,vert,horiz,ratio;

    angle=60;
    length=2;

    arads=angle*PI/180.0;
    vert=length*sin(arads);
    horiz=length*cos(arads);
    ratio=tan(arads);
    printf("Original angle = %9.6f\n",angle);
    printf("Vertical dist. = %9.6f\n",vert);
    printf("Horizon. dist. = %9.6f\n",horiz);
    printf("Ratio of sides = %9.6f\n",ratio);
    arads=atan(vert/horiz);
    angle=arads*180.0/PI;
    printf("Calculat angle = %9.6f\n",angle);
    length=hypot(vert,horiz);
    printf("Calcul. length = %9.6f\n",length);
}
```

On compiling and executing the program, C outputs

```
Original angle  =    60.000000
Vertical dist.  =     1.732051
Horizon. dist.  =     1.000000
Ratio of sides  =     1.732051
Calculat angle  =    60.000000
Calcul. length  =     2.000000
```

on the screen.

exp(x):
The exponential function raises the number e to the power of **x**. The **exp( )** function is the inverse of the **log( )** function. The relationship is

log(exp(x)) = x

log(x) and log10(x):
The logarithms to base e and base 10 are given by these functions. Antilogarithm functions are not given but they can easily be derived using the following identities:

Antilog(x)=e^x (base e. This is exp(x))
Antilog(x)=10^x (base 10)

abs(n), fabs(x) and labs(x):
The **abs( )** function returns the absolute (positive) value of a given integer number. For example **abs(12)** is 12, while **abs(–24)** is returned as 24.

The **fabs( )** function can be used to detect whether the values of two variables say, **x** and **y** (both declared of type **double**), are within an acceptable limit by using the statement in the form

```
if (fabs(x–y) < 0.00001)
    {
      execute these if true
    }
else
    {
      execute these if not true
    }
```

in which case the block of statements following the **if** statement will be executed only if the absolute difference of the two variables is less than the specified limit, indicating that they are approximately equal. We need to use the **fabs( )** function in the above statement otherwise a negative difference, no matter how small, would be less than the specified small positive number.

poly(x,n,c[ ]):
The **poly( )** function generates a polynomial in x, of degree n, with coefficients c[0], c[1], ..., c[n]. For example, if n=3, the generated polynomial is

$$c[3]x^3 + c[2]x^2 + c[1]x + c[0]$$

and **poly** returns the evaluated polynomial for the given x.

User-defined Functions

In some programs it may be necessary to use the same I/O process or mathematical expression in several places within the program, often using different data. C's user-defined functions enable definition of unique operations or expressions. These can then be called in the same manner as standard functions.

The user-defined function is identified by a call name followed by a parenthesized argument list, containing the parameters passed to the function from the main program. Functions must be defined using the following format:

```
[type value_returned] name(param1, param2, ...)
parameter declarations;
{
    local variable declarations;

    function statements;

    ----
    ----
    ----

    return(value);
}
```

Functions are usually defined after the end of the main program and several parameters, or none, can be passed to it. By definition, a function returns only one value and unless that value is of type **int**, we must declare the type returned as **float**, **double** or **char**. If the function is used to accomplish some process (such as printing a message), which does not return a value, then the function can be defined as type **void**.

Constants, data types, variables and function names which are declared outside of any function, including **main( )**, become *global*. This means that they can be used by any function in the program, including **main( )**, which follows their declaration.

Parameters must be declared immediately following the function definition. C does not permit direct access to the parameter values (unless pointers are used), but sends a copy of the parameter values to the function subprogram. What this means, of course, is that the function cannot change the values of these parameters, therefore only one value is returned from the function, via the **return(value)** statement which normally appears at the end of a function.

The exemption to this rule is when an array is passed to a function. The actual parameter is then a pointer to the first element in the array which means that the function can access and change the contents of the array directly.

Variables declared within a function are known as *local variables*. Their values or names are not known to other functions or indeed the main program.

The following program, which calculated the volume of a cylinder, illustrates the use of a user-defined function.

```
/* USER-DEFINED FUNCTION - VOLUME OF CYLINDER */
#include <math.h>
#define PI 3.141592654
double base( );

main( )
{
    double volume,height,radius,result;

    printf("Enter radius of cylinder ");
    scanf("%lf",&radius);
    printf("Enter height of cylinder ");
    scanf("%lf",&height);
    result=base(radius);
    volume=height*result;
    printf("\nResults from main program:\n");
    printf("Base area = %lf\n",result);
    printf("Volume = %lf\n",volume);
}

double base(r)                  /* Function definition  */

    double r;                   /* Parameter declaration */
    {
      double area;              /* Variable declaration  */

    area=PI*pow(r,2);
    printf("\nResults from within function:\n");
    printf("Radius squared = %lf\n",pow(r,2));
    printf("Area = %lf\n",area);

    return(area);
    }
```

Starting from the very top of the program, after the **#include** statement, constant **PI** is defined. By defining it outside the main program and all function subprograms, it implies that it can be used by any part of the program. Immediately following this, the compiler is informed that a function is to be used, by the name **base( )**, and that it is of type **double**. Then follows the main program with appropriate variable declarations.

Variable **radius** is the argument in the calling statement of function **base( )**, which causes a copy of the value held in the variable to be passed to the function through parameter **r**. There must be the same number of arguments in the call statement as there are parameters in the function definition, because there is a one to one correspondence between these two, although they don't have to have the same variable names.
If the first argument is of type **float**, then the first parameter must also be of type **float**, and so on.

Following the function definition, come the parameter declarations and then the function statements enclosed in braces. First amongst these statements are the local variable declarations which are to be known only to that function. Finally, note that the result of the calculation is **return**(ed) to the main program through a parenthesized variable (in this case, **area**), via the last statement in the function.

In this program you will find print statements liberally scattered in both the main program and the function. This was done on purpose so that the user can see the results from different parts of the program. When developing a program you should follow this example to make sure that what you think the function should return to the main program is actually what the function does return. It is a useful method by which to debug new program code.

Functions such as the user-defined function discussed above, are self-contained program units which can perform specific processes. Furthermore, as all parameters and local variables have no connection with similar quantities in other functions or the main program, it makes it easy and possible for us to build up a library of standard functions, which can then be used as building blocks to assemble new, lengthier programs.

Pointers and Functions

As stated previously, pointers can provide a method of changing the value of more than one variable from within a function. When ordinary variables are passed through the argument list of the call statement to the function via the parameters list, only a copy of the value of these variables is passed to the function. The function cannot alter the values of these variables because it is unaware where they are kept in memory. When, on the other hand, we use pointers, we are actually passing the address of the memory location where the variables are stored, therefore their value can be changed from within the function.

Pointers to Variables in Functions:

To illustrate the above point, the program below tests for the values held in two variables **a** and **b**. If the value in **a** is less that the value in **b** a function *swaps* the values of the two variables.

```
/* USING POINTERS TO VARIABLES IN FUNCTIONS */
void swap( );
main( )
{
    float a,b;

    printf("Enter two numbers: ");
    scanf("%f %f", &a, &b);
    if (a < b)
      swap(&a,&b);
    printf("\nRequired order is: %5.2f %5.2f\n",a,b);
}
void swap(pnta,pntb)
    float *pnta, *pntb;
    {
      float temp;

      temp = *pnta;
      *pnta = *pntb;
      *pntb = temp;
    }
```

Note that the function is defined as **void**, which means that there is no value to be returned. When entering the two variables **a** and **b**, we store the address (by using &) where their respective values are stored. The parameters within the function are then declared as pointers to the addresses where the values of **a** and **b** are to be found.

In this example, the statement **temp = *pnta;** should be interpreted as 'place the contents of memory location pointed to by ***pnta** into variable **temp**', while statement ***pnta = *pntb;** should be interpreted as 'place the contents of memory location pointed to by ***pnta** into the memory location pointed to by ***pntb**'. Thus, by using pointers we can change the contents of more than one location.

Pointers to Strings in Functions:

Similarly, we can use functions to manipulate strings by using pointers, as illustrated in the example below.

```
/* USING POINTERS TO STRINGS IN FUNCTIONS */
#include <stdio.h>
#include <alloc.h>
void swap( );
main( )
{
    char *name1, *name2;
    name1=(char *) malloc(9);
    name2=(char *) malloc(9);

    printf("Enter two names:  ");
    scanf("%s %s",name1, name2);
    if (strcmp(name1, name2) > 0)
     swap(&name1,&name2);
    printf("\nRequired order: %s %s\n", name1, name2);
}
void swap(pnta,pntb)
    char *(*pnta), *(*pntb);
    {
      char *temp;
      temp=(char *) malloc(9);

      temp = *pnta;
      *pnta = *pntb;
      *pntb = temp;
    }
```

The **char** declaration of ***pnta** and ***pntb** within function **swap( )** can be interpreted as 'pointers to pointers to character strings'. In this way we can swap the *addresses* of the strings (which are the values passed to the function), rather than having to swap each character of each string until the null (**0**) character is reached.

Pointers to Arrays in Functions:

When we pass a numeric array to a function, we actually pass a pointer to the first element of the array which means that we know where the elements of the array are stored in memory since they occupy contiguous locations. The following program allows us to input two floating point numbers into an array, it then examines them to see if they are in descending order (if not, it swaps them), and then prints them out. Note that the number of columns of **array[ ]** doesn't have to be declared within the function as it was already declared in the main program.

```
/* USING POINTERS TO ARRAYS IN FUNCTIONS */
void swap( );
#define COL 2
main( )
{
    float array[COL];
    int i;

    printf("Enter two numbers: ");
    for (i=0; i<COL; i++)
     scanf("%f",&array[i]);
    for (i=0; i<COL; i++)
     {
     if (array[0] < array[1])
       swap(array);
     }
    printf("\nRequired order is: ");
    for (i=0; i<COL; i++)
      printf("%5.2f",array[i]);
}
void swap(array)
     float array[];
     {
     float temp;

     temp = array[0];
     array[0] = array[1];
     array[1] = temp;
     }
```

Recursion

Functions can even call themselves; the technique is then called recursion. Recursion is simply a means of letting a function call itself. This can lead to some very elegant and efficient programs. The program listed below can be used to provide a conversion table from one currency to another. It is recursive, with the function calling itself many times until the problem is completed. This program is worth studying as recursive programming can be a very powerful technique once it is understood.

```
/* CURRENCY CONVERSION (RECURSIVE) */
#include <alloc.h>
float convert( );
float rate,result;
int max;
main( )
{
    char *name1,*name2;
    name1=(char *) malloc(9);
    name2=(char *) malloc(9);

    printf("Enter Currency 1: ");
    scanf("%s", name1);
    printf("Enter Currency 2: ");
    scanf("%s", name2);
    printf("Enter Exchange Rate: ");
    scanf("%f", &rate);
    printf("Enter Max Range: ");
    scanf("%d", &max);
    printf("\n%s\t %s\n",name1,name2);
    result=convert(max);
}
float convert(max)
    int max;
    {
    if (max > 0)
      {
      result=convert(max-1);
      result=max*rate;
      printf("%3d\t %5.2f\n",max,result);
      return(result);
      }
    return(0);
    }
```

Type in this program, save it under the filename **currency** and compile it. On execution, C asks you to give values to the four variables, after which it calculates and prints the answers.

```
Enter Currency 1: Pounds
Enter Currency 2: Dollars
Enter Exchange Rate: 1.54
Enter Max Range: 10
```

Pounds	Dollars
1	1.54
2	3.08
3	4.62
4	6.16
5	7.70
6	9.24
7	10.78
8	12.32
9	13.86
10	15.40

If we hadn't used recursion, we would have had to set up a loop to iterate through the required range. However, by using recursion, we have simplified the problem.

It is quite difficult to understand how the logic of a recursive procedure works at first. To illustrate the process, we shall look at the above example with **max=3**, indicating the flow of logic.

After the call statement in **main( )** the program diverts to the function **convert( )** with **max** set to 3. As **max** is greater than 0, program control passes to the next line within the function where the function is called again with **max=2**. Once more control is passed to the function definition statement after which there is another call to the function with **max=1**. Finally, this is repeated with **max=0**. At this point a change in the program flow takes place because **max** is equal to 0 so the **return(0)** statement is executed. The statement **result=** (on the line after the last function call) is then reached and the first line of the table is printed. There is now another end to the function with the **return(result)** statement so the program jumps to the line following the previous function call and the second line of the table is printed. This is repeated once more before control passes to the last statement of **main( )** where program execution ends.

```
        result=convert(max 3);
    }
float convert(max 3)
    {
        if (max > 0)
            {
            result=convert(max-1 2);
            result=max*rate;
            printf("%3d\t %5.2f\n",max,result);
            return(result);
            }
        return(0);
    }
float convert(max 2)
    {
        if (max > 0)
            {
            result=convert(max-1 1);
            result=max*rate;
            printf("%3d\t %5.2f\n",max,result);
            return(result);
            }
        return(0);
    }
float convert(max 1)
    {
        if (max > 0)
            {
            result=convert(max-1 0);
            result=max*rate;
            printf("%3d\t %5.2f\n",max,result);
            return(result);
            }
        return(0);
    }
float convert(max 0)
    {
        if (max > 0)
            {
            result=convert(max-1 0);
            result=max*rate;
            printf("%3d\t %5.2f\n",max,result);
            return(result);
            }
        return(0);
    }
```

Flow of logic in recursion

Problems

5.1 Newton's method of finding the square root of a number **x_val** is as follows:

(a) Make a guess at the square root, say **guess**. A good approximation for this could be built into the program as guess = x_val/2.

(b) Find **ratio** = **x_val/guess**

(c) Find the **average** of **ratio** and **guess**

(d) If **ratio** is approximately equal to **guess** (use the absolute floating point function in the statement if (fabs(ratio-guess) < 0.001), then the **average** in (c) gives a good approximation of the square root

(e) Otherwise, take the **average** as the new value of **guess** and repeat from (b).

Write a program capable of finding the square root of any number.

5.2 Modify the **bubble** program (to be found in Chapter 4) so that the actual swapping part of the bubble sorting routine is written as a function subprogram and is called as many times as it is necessary to sort a given list of numbers.

6. STREAMS & FILES

C, in line with the proposed ANSI standard, adopts the *buffered-file* system which is designed to work with a wide variety of internal and external devices. An internal file is a character array or character variable, and as such it is a sequential file; that is, the file is a sequence of character array elements, each one of which is a record. The order of the record is the same as the order of the array elements. All records have the same length, that of the array elements.

Most C device-files are external; that is, they are a physical device. Even though each device is different, the buffered-file system transforms each one into a logical device called a *stream*. Because streams are device (file) independent, the same functions that can write to the screen can also write to a disc file. There are two types of streams and two types of files.

Types of Streams and Files

The two types of streams are:

(a) text, which is a sequence of characters organized into lines that are terminated by a new line (\n) character, and

(b) binary, which is a sequence of bytes that have a one-to-one correspondence to those bytes in the external device.

The two types of file access are:

(a) sequential, for files associated with 'sequential devices', such as the keyboard, screen, printer, and data files created in sequential form, and

(b) random, for accessing disc files whose records can be read or written in any order.

A stream is associated with a specific file by the use of the library function **fopen( )**, which returns a *file pointer* which, if the file exists, it points to the beginning of the file. As each character is read from or written to the file, the file pointer is automatically incremented, to point to the next piece of information.

The format of **fopen( )** is as follows:

```
FILE *fptr, *fopen( );
fptr = fopen("filename", "mode");
```

where *filename* is a string associated with the name of the file, and *mode* can be one of the operations shown in the table below.

Table of Values of Mode

Symbol	Meaning
"r"	allows reading from a text file
"w	allows writing to a text file, but could overwrite existing data
"a"	allows data to be appended to the existing data of a text file
"rb"	allows reading from a binary file
"wb"	allows writing to a binary file, but could overwrite existing data
"ab"	allows data to be appended to the existing data of a binary file
"r+"	allows read/write from a text file
"w+"	creates a text file for reading/writing
"a+"	allows read/write or creates a text file
"r+b"	allows read/write from a binary file
"w+b"	creates a binary file for reading/writing
"a+b"	allows read/write or creates a binary file

Note that if a file opened in *write* or *append* mode does not exist, a file with the specified filename will be created on disc.

When the specified file in an **fopen( )** cannot be opened (for example as when an attempt is made to open a file in the *read* mode, and the file does not exist), a NULL (\0) character is returned. NULL is a macro that is defined in **stdio.h** header file.

To avoid fatal errors, program code should test for the return of NULL in the following way:

```
while ((fptr = fopen(filename,"r")) == NULL)
{
    printf("File could not be opened\n");
    exit(1);
}
```

A file can be disconnected from a specific stream by using a close operation. By closing a stream, the computer is forced to write any contents of the associated stream buffer to the external device. All files are automatically closed when a program terminates normally by **main( )** or by a call to **fclose( )** or **exit( )**. Files are not closed if the program ends abnormally through a crash. If that happens, you'll lose all information held in the buffer, but not what was already written to disc.

When a program first executes, the compiler opens three predefined streams. These are **stdin**, **stdout** and **stderr**. They normally refer to the standard I/O device, which is the console (keyboard and screen), and their *structure* is defined as of type **FILE** in the **stdio.h** header file. As C, however, allows *redirection*, these routines may be redirected to read or write to other devices, but must never be defined explicitly. The most common library file functions are listed below.

Table of Common Library File Functions

Name	Function
fopen( )	Opens a file
getc( )	Reads a character from a file
putc( )	Writes a character to a file
fseek( )	Seeks a specified byte in a file
fscanf( )	Scans a file for input
fprintf( )	Prints output to a file
feof( )	Returns **true** if **EOF** is reached
ferror( )	Returns **true** if an error occurs
rewind( )	Resets pointer to start of file
remove( )	Deletes the specified file
fclose( )	Closes a stream

Sequential Data Files

Most of the above library file functions are associated with sequential data files. To write data into such a file, we must use a small C program which will 'create' the file and then 'write' into it the data representing the information we would like to store on disc. The program below, which incorporates a few of the library functions listed previously, does this.

```c
/* WRITING TO AND READING FROM A FILE */
#include <stdio.h>
main( )
{
    int count,letter;
    char msg[20];
    FILE *fopen(), *fptr;

    if ((fptr=fopen("message.dat","w")) == NULL)
      {
      printf("Error in opening file\n");
      exit(1);
      }
    strcpy(msg,"Message to/from file");
    for (count=0; msg[count] !='\0'; count++)
      putc(msg[count],fptr);
    fclose(fptr);

    if ((fptr=fopen("message.dat","r")) == NULL)
      {
      printf("File cannot be opened\n");
      exit(1);
      }
    while ((letter=getc(fptr)) != EOF)
      putchar(letter);
    putchar('\n');
    fclose(fptr);
}
```

The above program (call it **fileio),** first opens a file by the name **message.dat** for writing (**"w"**), using the **fopen( )** function. If no errors occur, it first copies the message "Message to/from file" into character string **msg**, then the contents of **msg** are written character by character in the file, using the **putc( )** function, until character '\0' is encountered, signifying the end of the string, when the file is closed.

The file is then reopened for reading ("r") and the **getc( )** function is used to read its contents until the EOF (end of file) marker is encountered.

Command-line Arguments

It is often useful to pass information to a program when executing it, for example, passing the actual filename to the previous program, rather than having its name as part of the program code. This can be achieved by passing two special built-in arguments to the function **main( )**, namely **argc** and **argv**. These are the only arguments that **main( )** can have.

The **argc** parameter, which is an integer, holds the number of arguments on the command line which must be entered with a space between them. Parameter **argc** will always be at least 1, because the name of the program counts as the first argument. The **argv** parameter is a pointer to an array of character pointers, each element of which points to a separate command-line argument. The following program lines illustrate these points.

```
/* USING COMMAND-LINE ARGUMENTS */
#include <stdio.h>
main(argc,argv)
int argc;
char *argv[ ];
{
    int count,letter;
    char msg[20];
    FILE *fopen( ), *fptr;

    if (argc !=2)
      {
      printf("Filename required\n");
      exit(1);
      }
    if ((fptr=fopen(argv[1],"w")) == NULL)
      {
      printf("Error in opening file\n");
      exit(1);
      }

    ----
    ----   rest of the code
    ----

}
```

Note that parameters **argc** and **argv** must be declared immediately after **main( )** and before the opening brace of the main program. By declaring **argv** as an array, its individual arguments can be accessed by indexing.

Thus, **argv[0]** will point to the first string of the array, which is always the program's name; **argv[1]** will point to the second string of the array, which is the first argument of parameter **argv**.

Error and EOF Handling

C allows one program to execute another, in which case it is desirable for the calling program to check the status of functions from the executing program. There are two such mechanisms available; the **exit( )** function and the file pointer **stderr**.

The **exit( )** function (used previously) provides a method of terminating a program at a specific point. The function can return several values, the most common of which are 0 (for normal termination) or 1 (for abnormal termination) as used in the previous program to signify that the file had not been opened. These returned values can be examined by other calling program to check whether the program has been completed successfully before continuing with its own processing.

The **stderr** (standard error file) file pointer provides a mechanism for finding out whether an error has occurred in the two file pointers **stdin** and **stdout** when used to pipe output from one program as an input to another. Normally, if an error occurs within the first program, the error will not be sent to the screen, but will also be piped as input to the second program. To avoid such a situation happening we should use the **fprintf( )** function together with the file pointer **stderr** to display the error message on the screen. Function **fprintf( )** is similar to **printf( )**, but with the first argument being a file pointer to the destination of the output. The general form is:

```
fprintf(stderr, "Error has occurred %s\n", string);
```

which directs the error message to the display.

The final error trapping mechanism is the **feof( )** function. It was stated earlier that the buffered-file system can operate equally on text and binary data. However, when a binary file is opened for input, it is possible that the computer may interpret an integer value as the EOF.

The **feof( )** determines where the end-of-file marker is by taking a file-pointer argument and returning 1 if the end of file has been reached or 0 if it has not. Thus the loop

```
while ((letter=getc(fptr)) != EOF)
    putchar(letter);
    putchar('\n');
```

in our earlier program can be substituted by the loop

```
while (!feof(fptr))
    {
    letter=getc(fptr);
    putchar(letter);
    }
    putchar('\n');
```

which can also be adopted when reading text files.

File Read/Write Functions

In addition to the **putc( )** and **getc( )** functions used above, C provides several other functions which can be used to read from or write to a sequential device such as a stream or a file. For example, the functions **getw( )** and **putw( )** can be used to read and write integers from and to a file; they are similar to **putc( )** and **getc( )**, but instead of reading and writing a character, they read and write an integer. Another pair of functions is the **fgets( )** and **fputs( )** which can read and write strings from and to a stream; they are similar to **gets( )** and **puts( )**, but instead of reading and writing a string from and to the console, they read and write a string from and to a stream.

Perhaps the most useful buffered I/O functions are the **fread( )** and **fwrite( )**, which allow us to read and write blocks of data. They can be used as follows:

```
fread(value,sizeof(value),num,fptr);
fwrite(value,sizeof(value),num,fptr);
```

where, in the case of **fread( )**, **value** is a pointer to a memory region that will receive the data read from the file, while for **fwrite( )**, **value** is a pointer to the information that will be written to the file. In both cases, **num** represent 'number of times' each block of bytes given by **sizeof( )** will be accessed and **fptr** is the file pointer to a previously opened stream.

As long as the file is opened for binary data, **fread( )** and **fwrite()** can read and write any type of information. The following program, which is the solution to Problem 5.2 with several additions for file manipulation, is used to demonstrate the power of these functions. Save it under the filename **filesort**.

```
/* WRITE OUTPUT OF BUBBLE SORT */
/* TO EITHER SCREEN OR FILE */
#include <stdio.h>
#define COL 16
void swap( );

main(argc,argv)
int argc;
char *argv[ ];
{
    int value[COL];
    int i,j,temp,max,flag;
    char letter;
    FILE *fopen( ),*fptr;

    if (argc !=2)
     {
     printf("Output filenames required\n");
     exit(1);
     }
    printf("Enter the following %d numbers\n",COL);
    printf("7,6,1,9,7,14,39,24,19,32,21,8,5,15,28,4\n");
    printf("\nUnsorted list\n");
    for (i=0; i<COL; i++)
     scanf("%d",&value[i]);
    max=COL;
    for (i=0; i<COL-1; i++)
     {
     max=max-1;
     flag=0;
     for (j=0; j<max; j++)
      if (value[j] > value[j+1])
       {
       swap(value,j,max);
       flag=1;
       }
      if (flag == 0) break;
     }
    printf("Output to Screen or File (S/F) ");
    do
     letter=getchar( );
```

76

```
        while (letter != 'S' && letter != 'F');
        if (letter == 'S')
          {
           printf("\nSorted list\n");
           for (i=0; i<COL; i++)
             printf("%d ",value[i]);
          }
        else
          {
          if ((fptr=fopen(argv[1],"w+b")) == NULL)
          {
          printf("Error in opening file for output\n");
          exit(1);
          }
          printf("Writing sorted list to file\n");
          fwrite(value,sizeof(value),1,fptr);
          rewind(fptr);
          printf("Reading from file\n");
          fread(value,sizeof(value),1,fptr);
          fclose(fptr);
          for (i=0; i<COL; i++)
            printf("%d ",value[i]);
          }
  }
  void swap(value,index)
      int value[ ];
      int index;
      {
       int temp;

       temp = value[index];
       value[index] = value[index+1];
       value[index+1] = temp;
      }
```

The program asks you to enter a certain list of numbers which
are stored into array **value**. The contents of the array are then
sorted into ascending order using the **swap( )** user-defined
function, and the program then asks whether the output should
be directed to the screen or to the named file in the
command-line. If the user responds with **F**, the whole array is
written into the file, the pointer rewound, so that the contents of
the file are read into the array and subsequently displayed on the
screen.

File Scan/Print Functions

In addition to the buffered I/O functions introduced so far, two more will be discussed, namely the **fscanf( )** and **fprintf( )** which are particularly useful when we need to read from or write to a disc file assorted data types. The general form of declaration is:

```
fscanf(fptr,"control string",argument list);
fprintf(fptr,"control string",argument list);
```

where **fptr** is the file pointer returned by **fopen( )**. These functions act in the same manner as **scanf( )** and **printf( )**, except for directing output to the file defined by **fptr**.

The following program illustrates these functions. A file holds the name, telephone number and units used by each subscriber. The program can either add subscribers to the file, or interrogate the file by name for a subscriber, and if found, calculate and display the charges owed.

```
/* CHARGES FOR TELEPHONE SUBSCRIBERS */
#include <stdio.h>
#define COST 0.07
void newsubs( ),search( );
FILE *fopen( ),*fptr;

main(argc,argv)
int argc;
char *argv[ ];
{
    char ch;

    if (argc !=2)
     {-
     printf("Data filename required\n");
     exit(1);
     }
    if ((fptr=fopen(argv[1],"a+")) == NULL)
     {
     printf("File cannot be opened\n");
     exit(1);
     }
    do
     {
     printf("\nChoose (N)ew, (S)earch, or (Q)uit: ");
     ch=tolower(getche( ));
     printf("\n");
     }
```

```c
        while (ch != 'n' && ch != 's' && ch != 'q');
        if (ch == 'n')
          newsubs( );
        if (ch == 's')
          search( );
        if (ch == 'q')
          exit(1);
}
void newsubs( )
{
        char customer[15],number[10];
        int units;

        printf("Enter information on new customer\n");
        printf("\nName: ");
        fscanf(stdin,"%s",customer);
        printf("Phone No.: ");
        fscanf(stdin,"%s",number);
        printf("Units used: ");
        fscanf(stdin,"%d",&units);
        fprintf(fptr,"%s %s %d\n",customer,number,units);
        fclose(fptr);
}
void search( )
{
        char customer[15],name[15],number[10];
        int units;
        float charge;

        printf("Enter customer name: ");
        scanf("%s",name);
        while (!feof(fptr))
          {
          fscanf(fptr,"%s %s %d",customer,number,&units);
          if (stricmp(customer,name) == 0)
            {
            charge=COST*units;
            printf("\nCustomer: %s\n",customer);
            printf("Phone Num: %s\n",number);
            printf("Units used: %d\n",units);
            printf("Charge: £%5.2f\n",charge);
            break;
            }
          }
          fclose(fptr);
}
```

79

The program uses two user-defined functions, **newsubs( )** to add new subscribers to the file, and **search( )** to look up a given subscriber by name. The user is required to give the data file, say **customer.dat**, as a command line argument.

The data file is opened in the main part of the program for appending and reading after which a one line menu is displayed on the screen. The three options offered are **(N)ew, (S)earch** or **(Q)uit**. The program line following the display of the menu uses the **getche( )** function to get one only character from the keyboard (return is not required), and the **tolower( )** function, which converts the character entered to lower case. Thus, typing **N** or **n**, passes program control to function **newsubs( )**, while typing **S** or **s** passes program control to function **search( )**.

Note the use of **fscanf( )** within function **newsubs( )**. We use the automatically opened stream **stdin** as a file pointer to the keyboard, and print its contents, using **fprintf( )**, to the file pointed to by **fptr**. Also note that in function **search( )**, we use the case insensitive **stricmp( )** function to compare the entered name with those held in the file.

Type the program into your computer and create a simple list of subscribers, as given below.

Name	Phone Num	Units used
Smith	7141435	300
Jones	5743129	198
Adams	8466487	245
Brown	8673521	543

Use only single names and numbers without spaces, if the program is to work correctly.

Random Access Files

Records in a random-access file are numbered sequentially, with the first record as number 0, and all records have the same length, specified by the *offset* (in bytes) from a specified *origin* in the **fseek( )** function. Sequential data files, as we have used them up to now, can have different record lengths, and as such can occupy less space on disc. Records in a random access file can be read or written in any order by simply specifying the offset from the origin which can indicate the record number (or specific byte) to be read from or written to the file. The number of bytes written to a record must be less or equal to the record length.

The format of function **fseek( )**, used to place the file pointer at a specified location within the file is:

fseek(fptr, offset, origin);

where **fptr** is the file pointer returned by a call to **fopen( )**; **offset** is a *long* integer indicating the number of bytes required to reach the new position from a given *origin*; **origin** is one of the following integers:

Origin	Integer
start of file	0
current position	1
end of file	2

Once **fseek( )** has placed the file pointer in the required position, we can perform either read or write operations. The function **fseek( )** returns the value 0 if the operation was successful, or a negative value if an error occurred.

The following program, an adaptation of the previous one, illustrates some of the above points and introduces additional concepts. It requires you to create a telephone list, similar to that of the sequential file case (call it **telist.dta**), in which the names, telephone numbers and units used by each subscriber are part of the input. This file is then part of the command line input. Save the program under the filename **ranfile** (Random access Files).

```
/* TELEPHONE SUBSCRIBERS IN RANDOM FILE */
#include <stdio.h>
#define COST 0.07
#define SIZE 128

void newsubs( ),search( ),create( );
FILE *fopen( ),*fpdta;
long int offset,length;

main(argc,argv)
int argc;
char *argv[ ];
{
    char ch;

    if (argc !=2)
      {
       printf("Data filename required\n");
       exit(1);
      }
```

```
do
  {
   printf("\nChoose");
   printf("\n(N)ew, (S)earch, (C)reate, or (Q)uit: ");
   ch=tolower(getche( ));
   printf("\n");
  }
while(ch!='n' && ch!='s' && ch!='c' && ch!='q');
if (ch == 'n')
  {
   if ((fpdta=fopen(argv[1],"r+b")) == NULL)
     {
      printf("Data file cannot be opened\n");
      exit(1);
     }
   newsubs( );
  }
if (ch == 's')
  {
   if ((fpdta=fopen(argv[1],"rb")) == NULL)
     {
      printf("Data file cannot be opened\n");
      exit(1);
     }
   search( );
  }
if (ch == 'c')
  {
   if ((fpdta=fopen(argv[1],"wb")) == NULL)
     {
      printf("Data file cannot be opened\n");
      exit(1);
     }
   create( );
   fclose(fpdta);
   if ((fpdta=fopen(argv[1],"r+b")) == NULL)
     {
      printf("Data file cannot be opened\n");
      exit(1);
     }
   newsubs( );
  }
if (ch == 'q')
  exit(1);
}
```

```c
void newsubs( )
{
    char customer[15],number[10];
    int units,recnum;

    fscanf(fpdta,"%d",&recnum);
    printf("Records in File = %d\n",recnum);
    printf("Enter information on new customer\n");
    printf("\nName: ");
    fscanf(stdin,"%s",customer);
    printf("Phone No.: ");
    fscanf(stdin,"%s",number);
    printf("Units used: ");
    fscanf(stdin,"%d",&units);
    offset=(recnum+1)*SIZE;
    if (fseek(fpdta,offset,0))
      printf("Seek error\n");
    length=ftell(fpdta);
    printf("Pointer before writing at %ld\n",length);
    fprintf(fpdta,"%s %s %d\n",customer,number,units);
    recnum+=1;
    rewind(fpdta);
    fprintf(fpdta,"%d",recnum);
    fclose(fpdta);
}

void search( )
{
    char customer[15],name[15],number[10],ch;
    int units,recnum,searnum;
    float charge;

    fscanf(fpdta,"%d",&recnum);
    printf("Records in File = %d\n",recnum);
    do
      {
      printf("\nChoose");
      printf("\nBy (N)umber, or by (C)ustomer: ");
      ch=tolower(getche( ));
      printf("\n");
      }
    while(ch!='n' && ch!='c');
    if (ch == 'c')
      {
      printf("Enter customer name: ");
      scanf("%s",name);
      offset=0;
```

```c
    while (!feof(fpdta))
     {
       offset+=SIZE;
       if (fseek(fpdta,offset,0))
         printf("Seek error\n");
       fscanf(fpdta,"%s %s %d",customer,number,&units);
       if (stricmp(customer,name) == 0)
         {
         charge=COST*units;
         printf("\nCustomer: %s\n",customer);
         printf("Phone Num: %s\n",number);
         printf("Units used: %d\n",units);
         printf("Charge: £%5.2f\n",charge);
         break;
         }
       }
     }
    if (ch == 'n')
     {
       do
        {
          printf("Enter record number: ");
          scanf("%d",&searnum);
        }
       while(searnum > recnum);
       offset=searnum*SIZE;
       if (fseek(fpdta,offset,0))
         printf("Seek error\n");
       ftell(fpdta);
       printf("Pointer before reading at %ld\n",length);
       fscanf(fpdta,"%s %s %d",customer,number,&units);
       charge=COST*units;
       printf("\nCustomer: %s\n",customer);
       printf("Phone Num: %s\n",number);
       printf("Units used: %d\n",units);
       printf("Charge: £%5.2f\n",charge);
     }
    fclose(fpdta);
}

void create( )
{
    int recnum=0;

    fprintf(fpdta,"%d",recnum);
    printf("New file created\n");
}
```

84

The program keeps track of the number of records entered on the zeroth position of the file, with actual entries starting on the first record.

When you first start the program, (C)reate the data file by choosing option (C) from the menu. The file with the name given in the command argument list will then be initialized and you will be asked to enter the first record. New subscribers can be added to the list by rerunning the program and choosing the (N)ew option from the menu. As additional subscribers are added to the list, the information on the total number of records is updated.

Note the use of the statement **ftell(fpdta)**, which returns the position of the pointer from the origin of the file. Various print statements relating to the position of the pointer, either before writing to the file or before reading from the file, are incorporated in the program so that the user can get a feel of what is happening.

When you have created in this manner a list of several subscribers, use the (S)earch option of the menu to search for subscribers either by (C)ustomer name or by record (N)umber from a sub-menu of the (S)earch option. Do remember that the first customer is to be found in record 1, the second in record 2, and so on.

The program could be shortened considerably by the adoption of appropriate additional functions to deal with repetitive statements, as used at the beginning of the program to check whether the file could be opened or not. Try to add this facility.

Also, as an exercise, write an additional section to the program so that information already in the TELIST.DTA file can be edited, but make sure that the data file is opened with the **"r+b"** mode. Using any other mode can result in losing the information already in the file. Try it, you will learn a lot from this exercise.

Finally, C supports a second, unbuffered disc file I/O system, which uses functions that are slightly different from those of the buffered-file system. This second type of *low level* disc-file I/O system is similar to the Unix filing system. However, as the ANSI-standard committee has elected to standardise the buffered disc file I/O system and not the low level system, the latter is not dealt with in this book.

Problems

6.1 Modify the **fileio** program, appearing at the beginning of this chapter, so that it incorporates both command-line parameters (enabling the user to specify the name of the file to be written to or read from, as well as the mode of these operations) and the **feof( )** function (to allow binary files to be read correctly).

6.2 Modify the **filesort** program so that it can accept as input a list of employees which are then sorted in alphabetical order and can be written either onto the screen or into a sequential file. Save the program under the filename **employee**.

7. DEFINED DATA TYPES

C allows user definition of five different categories of data types. These are: Defining data types with the use of the **typedef** keyword, which creates a new name for an existing data type; Using the **typedef** keyword to define **enum** (enumerated) data types; **Structures**, which is a method of grouping related variables under a common name; **Unions**, which allows the use of the same area in memory by two or more different type of variables, and **bitfield**, which is a variation of the structure type and allows access to the individual bits within a byte.

The typedef Keyword

The **typedef** keyword allows the definition of a new name for an existing data type. The general form of the **typedef** statement is:

    typedef type name;

where *type* is any allowable data type and *name* is the new name chosen for this type. The name chosen by such a definition is in addition to, and not a replacement for, the existing data type.

For example, we could create a new name for **char** by using

    typedef char week;

which informs the compiler to recognise **week** as another name for **char**. Later on we could create a **char** variable by using **week** as follows:

    week day;

where **day** is now a character variable of type **week**.

Enumerated Data Types

An enumerated data type is implemented by C and is used to describe a discrete set of integer values. For example, we could declare the following:

    enum {Sun, Mon, Tue, Wed, Thu, Fri, Sat} days;

in a **typedef** definition. The names listed in **days** are integer constants with the first (Sun) being automatically set to zero, the second (Mon) set to one, and so on.

87

The following example will help to illustrate this type of definition. Note the declaration of variable **number** in the **main()** part of the program.

```
/* USING THE enum TYPE DEFINITION STATEMENT */
typedef enum { Sun,Mon,Tue,Wed,Thu,Fri,Sat } days;

main( )
{
    days number;

    printf("Which day number (0-6)? ");
    scanf("%d",&number);

    switch(number) {
      case 0: printf("Sunday"); break;
      case 1: printf("Monday"); break;
      case 2: printf("Tuesday"); break;
      case 3: printf("Wednesday"); break;
      case 4: printf("Thursday"); break;
      case 5: printf("Friday"); break;
      case 6: printf("Saturday"); break;
      default: printf("Not a day");
    }
}
```

Alternatively, the program can be written with the actual enumerated variables (Sun to Sat) appearing in the **case** statements of the **switch** command in place of the numbers 0 to 6, as follows:

```
    switch (number) {
      case Sun: printf("Sunday"); break;
      case Mon: printf("Monday"); break;
      case Tue: printf("Tuesday"); break;
      case Wed: printf("Wednesday"); break;
      case Thu: printf("Thursday"); break;
      case Fri: printf("Friday"); break;
      case Sat: printf("Saturday"); break;
      default: printf("Not a day");
    }
}
```

with the rest of the program, including the input to it, remaining identical to the previous version.

It is possible to override the automatic setting of variable **days** to the value from 0 onwards by specifying a particular value within the **enum** statement. For example, the statement could be used as shown below:

```
enum months {Apr=4, Jun=6, Sep=9, Nov=11};
```

to put in the correct monthly sequence all the months with 30 days, as shown below:

```
/* USING THE VALUED enum STATEMENT */
typedef enum { Apr=4, Jun=6, Sep=9, Nov=11 } months;

main( )
{
    months number;

    printf("Which month? (1-12) ");
    scanf("%d",&number);

    switch(number) {
      case 4: printf("April has 30 days"); break;
      case 6: printf("June has 30 days"); break;
      case 9: printf("September has 30 days"); break;
      case 11: printf("November has 30 days"); break;
      default: printf("Not a 30 day month");
    }
}
```

Note that a variable of an enumerated type can be assigned any value of type **int**, but must be within the range −32768 to 32767.

Structures

A structure is defined in C as a collection of variables that can be referenced under one name. They are equivalent to *records* in other high-level languages. You can think of a structure definition as a template that you may use to create structure variables. In general, all elements that make up a structure are logically related. For example, a list of customers with their telephone numbers can be declared as a structure. The **structure** definition is as follows:

```
struct subscriber {
    char name[20];
    char phone[15];
    int units;
};
```

Note the semicolon which terminates the definition. The reason for the existence of the semicolon is the fact that a **structure** is a statement. Further, the **structure** tag **subscriber** specifies the particular **structure**. To declare an actual **structure** variable **customer**, we can either use the definition

```
union subscriber customer;
```

or include the variable between the closing brace (}) and the semicolon which terminates the definition, as follows:

```
} customer;
```

Structure elements can be accessed by using the dot (.) operator as shown in the program segment below:

```
customer.units = 1234
```

where, for example, **customer.units** references the third element of the **structure**.

To print the number of units used by the specific customer we would write

```
printf("%d", customer.units);
```

which will print the **units** element of structure variable **customer**.

To access the **structure** variable through a pointer, as would be the case if we wanted to pass the address of an element of a structure to a function called **display( )**, we must use the **&** operator prior to the variable name, for example

```
display(&customer.units);
display(customer.phone);
```

Note that the **&** sign is not required in the second line as it is a string element. Also, within the function itself, we declare the argument as a pointer to the structure, as follows:

```
display(person)
struct subscriber *person;
```

and again we refer to individual elements of the structure with the dot notation, as follows:

    (*person).phone

Since structures are often passed to functions, C has a unique notation to describe pointers to structures. The notation -> is used in place of the dot notation. Thus, the previous reference can now be written as

    person -> phone

Arrays of Structures

The most common use of structures is perhaps in arrays of structures. To declare an array of structures, we first define a structure, and then declare an array variable of that type. For example, to declare a 50-element array of structures **subscriber** that was defined earlier, we write

    struct subscriber customer[50];

which creates 50 sets of variables that are organised in the same way as declared in the definition of structure **subscriber**.

To access a specific structure element, we index the structure name. For example, to print the number of units of structure 2, we write

    printf("%d%, customer[1].units);

which prints the third element (units) of the definition, but the second structure, as all structures, like arrays, begin their indexing at zero.

The example on the next page, will help to clarify all the points mentioned so far. However, in order to avoid having to retype all of the code of this program, you could modify the code of the "Charges for telephone subscribers" which appears under the section 'File Scan/Print Functions' of Chapter 6. Apart from the additional code, several changes have been made to the **main( )** part of the program, most of which deal with the appearance of the menu selection.

```c
/* CHARGES FOR TELEPHONE SUBSCRIBERS */

#include <stdio.h>
#define MAX 50
#define COST 0.07

struct subscriber {
    char name[25];
    char phone[15];
    int units;
    }customer[MAX];

void newsubs( ),search( ),file_it( ),load_it( );

main( )
{
    int i;
    char ch,filename[12];

    for (i=0; i<MAX; i++)
     *customer[i].name='\0';

    printf("Enter name of file: ");
    scanf("%s",filename);

    for(;;)
    {
     printf("\n(N)ewsubs:");
     printf("\n(S)earch:");
     printf("\n(F)ile_it:");
     printf("\n(L)oad_it:");
     printf("\n(Q)uit:\n\n");
     do
      {
      printf("Choose ... ");
      ch=tolower(getche( ));
      printf("\b\b\b\b\b\b\b\b\b\b\b\b");
      }
     while(!strchr("nsflq",ch));
     printf("\n");
     if (ch == 'n') newsubs( );
     if (ch == 's') search( );
     if (ch == 'f') file_it(filename);
     if (ch == 'l') load_it(filename);
     if (ch == 'q') exit(1);
    }
}
```

```c
void newsubs( )
{
    int i;

    for (i=0; i<MAX; i++)
     if(!*customer[i].name)
       break;
     if (i==MAX)
        {
        printf("Subscriber array full\n");
        return;
        }
     printf("Enter information on new customer\n");
     printf("\nName: ");
     scanf("%s",customer[i].name);
     printf("Phone No.: ");
     scanf("%s",customer[i].phone);
     printf("Units used: ");
     scanf("%d",&customer[i].units);
}

void search( )
{
    int i;
    float charge;
    char person[25];

    printf("Enter customer name: ");
    scanf("%s",&person);

    for (i=0; i<MAX; i++)
    {
     if (stricmp(customer[i].name,person) == 0)
     {
      charge=COST*customer[i].units;
      printf("\nCustomer: %s\n",customer[i].name);
      printf("Phone Num: %s\n",customer[i].phone);
      printf("Units used: %d\n",customer[i].units);
      printf("Charge: £%5.2f\n",charge);
      break;
     }
    }
}
```

```
void file_it(filename)
char filename[12];
{

    FILE *fopen( ),*fptr;
    int i;

if ((fptr=fopen(filename,"wb"))==NULL)
    {
      printf("File cannot be opened\n");
      return;
    }
    for (i=0;i<MAX; i++)
      if (*customer[i].name)
       if (fwrite(&customer[i], sizeof(struct subscriber),1,fptr)!=1)
         printf("Error while writing\n");
    fclose(fptr);
}
void load_it(filename)
char filename[12];
{
    FILE *fopen( ),*fptr;
    int i;

for (i=0; i<MAX; i++)
     *customer[i].name='\0';
    if ((fptr=fopen(filename,"rb"))==NULL)
     {
       printf("File cannot be opened\n");
       exit(1);
     }
    for (i=0; i<MAX; i++)
     if (fread(&customer[i], sizeof(struct subscriber),1,fptr)!=1)
      {
        if (feof(fptr))
         {
         fclose(fptr);
         return;
         }
         printf("Error while reading file\n");
      }
}
```

On starting the program, a structure called subscriber is defined and four functions are declared. These functions can respectively add new subscribers into memory, search the memory of a given subscriber, save the resultant database into the named file, or load into memory a previously filed database. Within the function **main( )**, the array **customer[ ].name** is initialised by placing in it a NULL (**'\0'**), which will be taken to signify an empty location into which we could add new subscribers later on.

Note the use of the **for(;;)** statement within **main( )** which sets up an infinite loop enclosing the menu statements. This allows us to consecutively load a file, add new subscribers to it, save it, search it, without exiting the program, which would result in loss of the information held in memory. This loop can only be abandoned by pressing q for quit, or by trying to load a non-existent file. Try it for yourself. Save the program under the filename **structure**.

Unions

A **union** is defined in C as a memory location which is used by several different variables, which can be of different types. The **union** definition is as follows:

```
union identity {
int id_number;
char_name[20];
float wages;
};
```

which is similar to the **struct** definition. The **union** tag **identity** specifies the particular **union**. To declare an actual **union** variable, say, **worker,** we use the definition

```
union identity worker;
```

In variable **worker**, the declared integer **id_number**, character **name[ ]** and floating point variable **wages** share the same memory location. Further, when a **union** is declared, C automatically creates a variable large enough to accommodate the largest variable in the **union**. Thus, using a **union** keeps your program code independent of the machine in which it is being used as the compiler itself keeps track of the sizes of the variables that make up the **union**.

95

Union elements can be accessed by using the dot (.) operator as shown in the program segment below:

```
if (worker == number)
    printf("%d\n", identity.id_number);
if (worker == surname)
    printf("%c\n", identity.name);
if (worker == earnings)
    printf("%f\n", identity.wages);
```

where, for example, **identity.name** references the second element of the **union**.

To access the **union** variable through a pointer, as would be the case if we wanted to pass the address of an element of a union to a function called **display( )**, we must use the **&** operator prior to the variable name, for example

```
display(&worker.id_number);
```

and within the function itself we must declare the argument as a pointer to the union, as follows:

```
display(person)
union identity *person
```

Thus, unions should be viewed as simple variations of structures which we have already discussed.

Bitfields

A unique feature in C, based on structures, is its ability to access a single bit within a byte. This can be useful when trying, for example, to control external devices. Although most of the operations accessible through bitfields can also be performed with bitwise operators, the adoption of a bitfield can add more structure to a program code. The general form of a bitfield definition is

```
struct device_name {
    type name1 : length;
    type name2 : length;
    ...
    ...
} code;
```

Bitfields must be declared as either **int**, **signed** or **unsigned**, with those of length 1 as **unsigned**.

As the application of bitfields is rather specialised and only of interest to relatively few people, we will not pursue it any further. Those interested should refer to more advanced books in C.

Linked Lists

In our previous example, lists of subscribers were either created in memory or loaded from a file into memory, but at all times we used an array of **MAX** dimension to hold our list. This can be wasteful in terms of memory usage. Once the list grows beyond the defined size, we must increase its size. C provides an answer, in the form of linked lists, which can help to eliminate this wastage of memory space. Linked lists can dynamically grow or shrink to hold exactly the correct, but minimum, number of records.

Linked lists utilise the ability of a member of a structure to be a pointer to a structure of the same type as the one in which it is itself contained. For example, using our telephone subscribers list, we could incorporate a pointer to point to the next subscriber, as follows:

```
struct subscriber {
    char name[25];
    char phone[15];
    int units;
    struct subscriber *forth;
};
```

where the first subscriber in the list points **forth** to the second, the second to the third, and so on, with the last pointing to the value NULL. Additional subscribers can be inserted between the last subscriber and the value NULL.

When first creating a linked list, a pointer should be assigned to point to the start of the list, as follows:

```
struct subscriber *customer, *start;
if ((customer = (struct subscriber *)
     calloc(1,sizeof(struct subscriber)))==NULL)
    {
    printf("No available memory for allocation\n");
    exit(1);
    }
customer -> forth = NULL
start = customer;
```

We can then assign values to the first subscriber in the usual way. For example,

```
printf("Enter information on new customer\n");
printf("\nName: ");
scanf("%s",customer->name);
printf("Phone No.: ");
scanf("%s",customer->phone);
printf("Units used: ");
scanf("%d",&customer->units);
```

Linked lists are very powerful, but difficult for many programmers to thoroughly understand. Furthermore, as the application of linked lists is rather specialised and only of interest to those relatively few who intend to write their own database, we will not pursue this vast and complex subject any further.

Apart from linked lists, C provides several other methods for dealing with lists of information, such as queues, stacks, and binary trees. Those interested in these, as well as on how to use system resources in order to control the screen of their display - including the ability of using graphics, keyboard or other attached peripheral devices, should refer to books which deal specifically with these subjects as the depth and complexity of the required knowledge is beyond the scope of introductory books such as this.

However, having said this, controlling system resources, such as the screen and the keyboard, or using graphics, is made extremely simple with Borland's Turbo C, Version 1.5 compiler with its built-in functions. These are not pursued in this book for two reasons; (a) they are well covered by Borland's User Guide Supplement, (b) they are not supported by other C compilers.

Problem

7.1 After you have examined the code of the **structure** program and have understood it thoroughly, incorporate a sixth menu option to the program which can display the names and associated phone numbers of all the subscribers in the list. Call this function **display( )**.

APPENDIX A

THE ED LINE EDITOR

UNIX provides you with its own simple line editor, called **Ed** - the subject of this appendix, and you should become familiar with its use, if UNIX is your particular environment.

If, on the other hand, you are using the DOS environment, then you have a wider choice of editors, such as the full screen editor **Edit** which is available to users of DOS 5 and beyond, or the line editor **Edlin** which is the only one available to pre-DOS 5 users. Further, if you are using either Microsoft's or Borland's C compilers, then you also have the particular package's editor at your disposal. As these editors are all different, they will not be covered in this book as the space required to describe them all will be out of proportion to the total number of pages in the book.

In general, **Ed** and the other editors allow the creating and editing of ASCII files. These are text files which when sent to the screen or printer are interpreted as text. Such editors can also be used to create the source code of various programming languages, such as C and Fortran. In such cases, you should remember to give your source file the appropriate extension. For the two languages mentioned above, these will be **.c** and **.for**, respectively.

Invoking the ED Line Editor

To invoke **Ed**, the UNIX System disc or a disc that contains it must be in the logged drive, and the file you want to create or edit must be specified. Thus, typing the command:

    $ ed test.txt

expects to find both **Ed** and the fictitious file **test.txt** on the disc in the logged directory (in this case $), while typing

    $ ed c:test.txt

expects to find **Ed** on the disc in the logged drive and the file **test.txt** on the disc in the **c:** drive.

If the file does not exist on the specified disc drive, then **Ed** responds with

    ? test.txt

The query (?) is **Ed**'s response to instructions it does not expect (in this case because the file does not exist) and waits for further commands.

If the file already exists, then **ed** loads the file into RAM and responds with a number indicating the file's size in bytes, for example

    321

Let us now create a text file, called **test.txt**, which we will use to demonstrate the power of **ed**. To start, type at the prompt the command

    $ ed test.txt

which should cause **ed** to respond with

    ? test.txt

if that file does not exist on your disc or directory. If it does exist and you do not want to spoil its contents, then type **q** (for quit) and press the Return key.

The Append Command:
To append lines of text, use the command **a** (for append). In the case of a new file, as no lines of text exist in the file, type **a** and then type in the short text given below, pressing the Return key at the end of each line.

    a
        first line of text
        second line of text
        third line of text
        fourth line of text
        .

The contents between **a** and . (dot), are appended to the empty file. As **ed** does not give any prompt at all, the text given above is exactly what you see on the screen. The dot ends the appending mode and also marks the last line of text (in this case line 4), as the *current line*. The current line is also known as the *dot* line, but still refers to the last line of text to be entered, changed or listed. To find out which line is the current (or dot) line, type 'n' which will display its number. Typing '.', will display the contents of the current line, while '$=' displays the number of the very last line in the file.

The List Command:
To see what text is in the file, type l (for list), as follows:

```
l
    fourth line of text
```

The line listed by **ed** is the current line (the last line of text appended previously).

To list specific lines, use the l command with line numbers. For example,

```
1,3l
```

will list lines from 1 to 3 inclusive, while

```
2,$l
```

will list lines from 2 to the end of file, as the $ symbol is taken to mean "end of file".

Note the command syntax which is: "From start number to end number list". There must be no comma between the second line number and the command letter. Also note that listing lines causes the 'current line' to be changed to the last listed line.

The Write Command:
Created text can be saved to disc by writing it to file, using the **w** command. Thus, typing

```
w
```

will cause the above two lines of text to be written to the **test.txt** file.

From that point on, you could quit **ed** by typing

```
q
```

Had the text not been written to file or edited in any way since the last write to file, **ed** will respond with

```
?
```

and replying by pressing **q** again, will quit the editor with consequent loss of information.

The Change Command:

To change a specific line of text, type its number, followed by **c** (for change), which first deletes from the buffer the contents of the line to be changed. If the line number is omitted then it is assumed that you intend to change the current line. In either case, this puts you in the change mode and anything you type will replace the intended line.

In our case, we want to change line 2 to

   second line of text, edited

  so, enter the change mode by typing

  2c

and change the line appropriately by re-typing it and typing '.' (dot) to terminate the change mode.

The Insert Command on an Existing File:

To insert lines of text, use the command **i** (for insert). However, be warned. Using **i** by its own will insert the new line *before* the current line. To insert lines at any other point, give the line number before the command.

  In our case, we would like to insert one additional line in between the first two lines. To do this, type

  2i
       in between line

     .

Again, insertion mode is terminated by typing a dot. If we now list the first three lines of the file, we get:

  1,3l
  first line of text
  in between line
  second line of text, edited

Note that the last line to be inserted becomes the current line (in this case line 2) which was the case prior to issuing the list command, after which line 3 becomes the current line as it is the last line to be listed.

The Delete Command:

To delete unwanted lines of text, use the **d** command (for delete). However, if you use the **d** command without any number associated with it, you will delete the current line. Therefore, if you want to delete line 2, say, type

2d

or if you want to delete a group of lines, type

13,15d

which is translated as "lines 13 to 15 to be deleted". If the range given is beyond the file-end, **ed** responds with its usual '?'.

The Move and Transcribe Commands:

To move or transcribe (copy) text, use the **m** or **t** commands (for move or transcribe). These commands must be preceded by numbers, as follows:

13,15m8
13,15m$

which is interpreted as "lines 13 to 15 to be moved to a position *after* line 8", and "lines 13 to 15 to be moved to the end of the file", respectively. If the range given is beyond the file-end, **ed** responds with its usual '?'.

Similarly, the **t** command will transcribe a block and insert it *after* the given line. To move or transcribe a single line, precede the command with only one number. If the command letter is given without a leading line number, **ed** assumes you want to operate on the current line.

The Search Command:

To search for the occurrence of a word or a specified number of characters in a file you have created using **ed**, use the search command. Just as in the list and delete commands, a line range could be specified, followed by the string to be searched for in slashes. The command

/edited/

will start a search for 'edited' from the current line to the end of the file, and if it does not find a match, it will continue from the beginning of the file.

Thus, each line of the file is searched forwards from the current line. When a match is found, the contents of the matched line are displayed. Typing 'n', will give its line number.

The search command finds only the first occurrence of the specified string. To continue the search for further occurrences of the same string, simply type

```
//
```

again, as **ed** remembers the last pattern used. Thus, typing

```
/ir/
first line of text
//
third line of text
```

causes **ed** to first find the string 'ir' in the word 'first' of line 1, then by typing //, it displays the second occurrence of the same string 'ir' in the word 'third' of line 3. However, pressing the Return key, displays the contents of the next numbered line in the file irrespective of search pattern.

The Substitute Command:
This command is similar to the search command, except that it requires the **s** command and a replacement string. Thus, typing

```
1,4s/edited/re-edited/
```

will cause the *first* occurrence of the word 'edited' within the specified line range of text, to be replaced by the word 're-edited'. Here, of course, it occurs once in line 2 of the text.

If you want to substitute <u>all</u> occurrences of the specified string by another within the given range, then use the **g** (for global) option, as follows:

```
1,4s/edited/re-edited/g
```

If only one line number is specified before the **s** command, only that line will be affected. Further, the command

```
s/re-//
```

will replace the word 're-' by nothing, effectively deleting it, provided the characters 're-' are to be found on the current line, otherwise **ed** will respond with '?'.

Similarly, the **&** option could be used to insert characters either before or after a specified string, depending on the position of the **&**. For example,

```
s/line/&d/
s/line/under&/
```

will replace the string 'line' with 'lined' in the first case, and 'line' with 'underline' in the second case.

Exiting ed

To end the current session and exit **ed** at any point, type

```
w
```

which writes to disc the contents of the file under the chosen filename, then type

```
q
```

to quit the editor.

If, on the other hand, you realised that too many mistakes were made during editing, you could use the **q** command to quit **ed**, but without first writing to disc with the **w** command. This will invoke the

```
?
```

response, to which you will have to reply by pressing **q** again.

Ed supports a wealth of extra commands which were not discussed above. The commands presented are more than adequate for writing and editing all but the most difficult programs within the UNIX environment. If you intend to write complicated programs which might require extensive editing, then it is best to use a full screen editor such as **Vi**.

APPENDIX B

Solutions

Problem 1.1

```
/* DAYS & HOURS TO MINUTES CONVERSION */
main( )
{
    float days,hours,minutes,total;

    printf("Enter number of days:  ");
    scanf("%f",&days);
    printf("Enter number of hours:  ");
    scanf("%f",&hours);
    printf("Enter number of minutes:  ");
    scanf("%f",&minutes);
    total=24*60*days+60*hours+minutes;
    printf("Total number of minutes are %f",total);
}
```

Problem 1.2

```
/* TEMPERATURE CONVERSION FROM °F TO °C */
#define FACTOR 5/9
main( )
{
    float f,c;

    printf("Enter degrees Fahrenheit:  ");
    scanf("%f",&f);
    c=(f-32.0)*FACTOR;
    printf("Degrees Celsius = %f",c);
}
```

Problem 2.1

```
/* INTEGRAL AND FRACTIONAL PARTS OF A NUMBER */
main( )
{
    float value,fractional;
    int integral;

    printf("Enter a value ");
    scanf("%f",&value);
    integral=value;
    fractional=value-integral;
    printf("\nOriginal\t Integral\t Fractional\n");
    printf("%f\t %d\t\t %f",value,integral,fractional);
}
```

Problem 2.2

```
/* COST OF ELECTRICITY */
#define UNIT_COST 5.5
#define FLAT_RATE 885.0
main( )
{
    float low_value,hi_value,cost,frate,ucost;
    int units;

    frate=FLAT_RATE/100;
    printf("Enter last quarter's meter reading: ");
    scanf("%f",&low_value);
    printf("Enter this quarter's meter reading: ");
    scanf("%f",&hi_value);
    units=hi_value - low_value;
    ucost=units*UNIT_COST/100;
    cost=ucost + FLAT_RATE/100;
    printf("\nUnits used  :%7d",units);
    printf("\nUnits cost  :£%6.2f",ucost);
    printf("\nFlat rate   :£%6.2f",frate);
    printf("\nTotal cost  :£%6.2f",cost);
}
```

Problem 3.1

```
/* GRADING EXAMINATION RESULTS */
main( )
{
    int number, mark;

    printf("Enter candidate number:  ");
    scanf("%d",&number);
    while (number >= 0 && number <= 32767)
      {
        printf("Enter exam mark: ");
        scanf("%d",&mark);
        printf("\nNumber\t Mark\t Grade\n");
        if (mark >= 70 && mark <= 100)
          printf("%d\t %d\t %c\n",number,mark,'A');
        else if (mark >= 60 && mark < 70)
          printf("%d\t %d\t %c\n",number,mark,'B');
        else if (mark >= 50 && mark < 60)
          printf("%d\t %d\t %c\n",number,mark,'C');
        else if (mark >= 40 && mark < 50)
          printf("%d\t %d\t %c\n",number,mark,'D');
        else if (mark >= 0  && mark < 40)
          printf("%d\t %d\t %c\n",number,mark,'F');
        printf("\nEnter candidate number:  ");
        scanf("%d",&number);
      }
}
```

Problem 3.2

```c
/* COMPOUND INTEREST */
#define MAX_YEARS 15
main( )
{
    int n,k;
    float rate=11.5;
    float money_lent=5000.00;
    float result,value,amount;

    value=1+rate/100;
    for (n=1; n<=MAX_YEARS; n++)
      {
        result=1.0;                             /* routine to */
        for (k=1; k<=n; k++)                     /*    raise   */
          {                                      /*   'value'  */
            result=result*value;                 /*   to the   */
      }                                          /* power of n */
            amount=money_lent*result;
            printf("%10d %15.2f %15.2f\n",n, result, amount);
          }
}
```

Problem 4.1

```c
/* GENERAL STRING SORTING PROGRAM */
#include <alloc.h>
#include <string.h>
#define MAX_NUM 4
#define MAX_LEN 6
main( )
{
    int i,j,k;
    char *names[MAX_NUM], *temp;

    for (i=0; i<MAX_NUM; i++)
      names[i]=(char *) malloc(MAX_LEN);
    temp=(char *) malloc(MAX_LEN);
    printf("Enter %d names, each of\n",MAX_NUM);
    printf("%d characters in length\n",MAX_LEN);
    printf("\nUnsorted list\n");
    for (i=0; i<MAX_NUM; i++)
      {
      printf("%d ",i+1);
      gets(names[i]);
      }
    for (i=0; i<MAX_NUM-1; i++)
      {
      for (j=0; j<MAX_NUM-1; j++)
        if (strcmp(names[j], names[j+1]) > 0)
          {
            temp=names[j];
            names[j]=names[j+1];
            names[j+1]=temp;
          }
      }
    printf("\nSorted list\n");
    for (k=0; k<MAX_NUM; k++)
      puts(names[k]);
}
```

Problem 4.2

```
/*FIBONACCI SERIES */
#include <stdio.h>
#define COL 12

main( )
{
    int series[COL], i;
    float sum[COL-1];

    series[0]=1;
    series[1]=1;
    for (i=2; i<COL; i++)
      series[i]=series[i-2]+series[i-1];

    for (i=0; i<COL-1; i++)
      sum[i]=((float)series[i]+(float)series[i+1])/2.0;

    printf("Fibonacci series is:\n");
    for (i=0; i<COL; i++)
      printf("%6d",series[i]);

    printf("\nAverages of adjacent terms is:\n");
    for (i=0; i<COL-1; i++)
      printf("%6.1f",sum[i]);
}
```

Problem 5.1

```c
/* NEWTON'S METHOD OF FINDING SQUARE ROOTS */
#include <math.h>
#define MAX_ITER 50
main( )
{
    double xval,guess,ratio,aver;
    int i;

    printf("Enter a number: ");
    scanf("%lf",&xval);
    printf("Guess a value : ");
    scanf("%lf",&guess);
    printf("\nIter\t  Average\n");
    for (i=0; i<MAX_ITER; i++)
      {
      ratio=xval/guess;

      aver=(ratio+guess)/2.0;
      printf("%d\t %9.5lf\n",i,aver);
      if (fabs(ratio-guess) < 0.0001)
        {
        printf("\nSquare root of %9.5lf ",xval);
        printf(" = %9.5lf\n",aver); break;
        }
      else
        guess=aver;
      }
      if (i==MAX_ITER-1)
        {
        printf("Not converging in %d ",MAX_ITER);
        printf("Iterations\n");
        }
}
```

Problem 5.2

```c
/* BUBBLE SORT TECHNIQUE WITH SWAP FUNCTION */
#include <stdio.h>
#define COL 16
void swap( );

main( )
{
    int value[COL];
    int i,j,temp,max,flag;

    printf("Enter the following %d numbers\n\n",COL);
    printf("7,6,1,9,7,14,39,24,19,32,21,8,5,15,28,4\n");
    printf("\nUnsorted list\n");
    for (i=0; i<COL; i++)
      scanf("%d",&value[i]);
    max=COL;
    for (i=0; i<COL-1; i++)
      {
       max=max-1;
       flag=0;
       for (j=0; j<max; j++)
        if (value[j] > value[j+1])
          {
           swap(value,j,max);
           flag=1;
          }
        if (flag == 0) break;
      }
      printf("\nSorted list\n");
      for (i=0; i<COL; i++)
        printf("%d ",value[i]);
}
void swap(value,index)
    int value[ ];
    int index;
    {
    int temp;

    temp = value[index];
    value[index] = value[index+1];
    value[index+1] = temp;
}
```

114

Problem 6.1

```c
/* WRITING TO AND READING FROM A FILE */
#include <stdio.h>
#include <alloc.h>
main(argc,argv)
int argc;
char *argv[ ];
{
    int count;
    char *msg,letter;
    FILE *fopen( ),*fptr;

    msg=(char *) malloc(50);

    if (argc !=3)
      {
        printf("Filename & Mode required\n");
        exit(1);
      }
    if ((fptr=fopen(argv[1],argv[2])) == NULL)
      {
        printf("\nError in opening file\n");
        exit(1);
      }
    printf("Enter message: ");
    gets(msg);
    printf("\nWriting to disc\n");
    for (count=0; msg[count] !='\0'; count++)
      putc(msg[count],fptr);
    fclose(fptr);

    printf("\nReading from disc\n");
    if ((fptr=fopen(argv[1],"r")) == NULL)
      {
      printf("File cannot be opened\n");
      exit(1);
      }
    printf("Message is: ");
    while (!feof(fptr))
      {
      letter=getc(fptr);
      putchar(letter);
      }
    putchar('\n');
    fclose(fptr);
}
```

Problem 6.2

```c
/* SORTING LISTS OF EMPLOYEES */
#include <alloc.h>
#include <stdio.h>
#define NUM 5
#define LEN 6
void swap( );
void rewind( );

main(argc,argv)
int argc;
char *argv[ ];
{
    char *employee[NUM];
    int i,j,max,flag;
    char letter;
    FILE *fopen( ),*fptr;

    if (argc !=2)
      {
      printf("Output filenames required\n");
      exit(1);
      }
    for (i=0; i<NUM; i++)
      employee[i]=(char *) malloc(LEN);
    printf("Enter the names of %d employees\n",NUM);
    printf("\nUnsorted list\n");
    for (i=0; i<NUM; i++)
      gets(employee[i]);
    max=NUM;
    for (i=0; i<NUM-1; i++)
      {
      max=max-1;
      flag=0;
      for (j=0; j<max; j++)
        if (strcmp(employee[j], employee[j+1]) > 0)
          {
          swap(employee,j,max);
          flag=1;
          }
        if (flag == 0) break;
      }
    printf("\nOutput to Screen or File (S/F) ");
```

```
      do
        letter=getchar( );
      while (letter !='S' && letter != 'F');
      if (letter == 'S')
        {
        printf("\nSorted list\n");
        for (i=0; i<NUM; i++)
          printf("%s\n",employee[i]);
        }
      else
        {
        if ((fptr=fopen(argv[1],"w+b")) == NULL)
        {
        printf("Error in opening file for output\n");
        exit(1);
        }
        printf("\nWriting sorted list to file\n");
        fwrite(employee,sizeof(employee),1,fptr);
        rewind(fptr);
        printf("\nReading from file\n");
        fread(employee,sizeof(employee),1,fptr);
        fclose(fptr);
        for (i=0; i<NUM; i++)
          printf("%s\n",employee[i]);
        }
}
void swap(employee,index)
      char *employee[ ];
      int index;
      {
        char *temp;

        temp = employee[index];
        employee[index] = employee[index+1];
        employee[index+1] = temp;
      }
```

Problem 7.1

Statements that need to changed in function main( ) of the STRUCT program are identified with the plus (+) symbol which appears in the first column of the listing below.

The code for the function display( ) is shown in its entirety.

```
/* CHARGES FOR TELEPHONE SUBSCRIBERS */

#include <stdio.h>
#define MAX 50
#define COST 0.07

struct subscriber {
    char name[25];
    char phone[15];
    int units;
    }customer[MAX];

+   void newsubs( ),search( ),display( ),file_it( ),load_it( );

    main( )
    {
    int i;
    char ch,filename[12];

    for (i=0; i<MAX; i++)
        *customer[i].name='\0';

    printf("Enter name of file: ");
    scanf("%s",filename);

    for(;;)
    {
    printf("\n(N)ewsubs:");
    printf("\n(S)earch:");
+   printf("\n(D)isplay:");
    printf("\n(F)ile_it:");
    printf("\n(L)oad_it:");
    printf("\n(Q)uit:\n\n");
    do
     {
     printf("Choose ... ");
     ch=tolower(getche( ));
     printf("\b\b\b\b\b\b\b\b\b\b\b");
     }
```

```
+      while(!strchr("nsdflq",ch));
       printf("\n");

       if (ch == 'n') newsubs( );
       if (ch == 's') search( );
+      if (ch == 'd') display( );
       if (ch == 'f') file_it(filename);
       if (ch == 'l') load_it(filename);
       if (ch == 'q') exit(1);
    }
}

void display( )
{
    int i;

    for (i=0; i<MAX; i++)
    {
     if (*customer[i].name)
       {
       printf("%s\t",customer[i].name);
       printf("%s\n",customer[i].phone);
       }
     }
}
```

INDEX

A

abs() function 55, 58
Accumulator 18
acos() function 55, 56
Addition 11
Address operator . 15, 19, 41
alloc() function 41
Ampersand (&) 6, 15, 19
AND (&&) logical operator 17
ANSI standard 85
Append file mode 70
argc 73
Argument 6
  command line 73
argv 73
Arithmetic
  operators 5, 11
  priority 11, 23
  symbols 5, 11
Arrays 15
  declaration 15, 50
  numerical 49
  pointers 39
  strings 43
ASCII
  characters 14
  codes 46
  files 1
asin() function 55, 56
Assignment statement . 6, 11
Asterisk (*) 19, 41
atan() function 55, 56
atof() function 55
atoi() function 55
atol() function 55

B

Backslash 14
Binary data 21
Bitfield 96
Bitwise operators 20
Boolean
  true 17
  false 17
Borland's Turbo C
  compiler 7
  resource control 98
Braces 2
break statement 34
Bubble sort 51
Buffered-file system 69

C

calloc() function 97
case() function 36
char type 3, 15
Character
  array 15, 39
  definition 39
  I/O 13, 15
  pointers 39, 41
  string 39
Combined operators 22
Command-line argument . 73
Comments 2
Compiling 7
Concatenation 47
Conditional operators 25
Constant declaration 5
continue statement 34
Control program flow 25
cos() function 55, 56
cosh() function 55

D

Data files
  random access 69, 80
  sequential 69, 72
Data type 3
  arrays 15
  constants 5
  conversion 4
  definition 5
  initialisation 1
  qualifiers 3
  register 33
  variables 2
Decimal numbers 3
Declaration
  arrays 49
  constants 5
  variables 2, 3
Decrement operator (—) .. 19
default statement 36
define
  statements 5, 15
  data types 87
Division 11
do-while loop 28
Dot notation 91
double type 3

E

ecvt() function 55
Ed line editor 99
else statement 26
enum type 87
Enumeration 87
EOF 74
Equality operator (==) 17
Error handlers 74
Escape sequences 14
Evaluation of expressions . 11
.EXE files 8
Executable files 7, 8

exit() function 71
exp() function 55, 57
Expressions 5, 10

F

fabs() function 55, 58
fclose() function 71
feof() function 71, 75
ferror() function 71
FILE type 7, 69
File
  descriptor 70
  error handlers 74
  Input/Output mode 70
  random access 69, 80
  pointers 69
  sequential 69, 72
  stderr 71, 74
  stdin 71, 74
  stdio.h header 15, 71
  stdout 71, 74
float type 3
Floating point values 3
Flow of control 25
  break 34
  continue 34
  goto 33
  if 25
  if-else 26
  iterative statements 27
  switch 35
fmod() function 55
fopen() function 69, 71
for loop 29
  nested 32
for (;;) infinite loop 35, 95
Format
  controls 13
  specifications 6
Formatted output 12, 13
fprintf() function ... 71, 74, 78

fread() function 75
fscanf() function 71, 78
fseek() function 71, 80
Functions
  arguments 56, 59
  library 71
  pointers 62, 63
  recursion 65
  variables 60
fwrite() function 75

G
getc() function 71
getchar() function . 16, 29, 35
getche() function 78
gets() function 15
Global variables 59
goto statement 33

H
Header files 15
Hexadecimal numbers 13, 20
Hyperbolic functions 55
hypot() function 55, 56

I
if statement 25
if-else statement 26
  nested 27
include statement 5, 15
\INCLUDE subdirectory 8
increment operator (++) ... 18
Indirection operator (*) 19, 41
Inequality operator (!=) ... 17
Infinite looping 35, 95
Initialisation 4
Input/Output (I/O)
  field types 13
  formatted 12
  priority 11
  stream 6

int type 3
Integer
  definition 5
  division 16
  variables 3

J
Join strings 47

K
Keywords 3, 4

L
Label 33, 34
labs() function 55, 58
\LIB subdirectory 8
Line editor ed 99
Linked lists 97
Local variables 60
log() function 55, 58
log10() function 55, 58
Logical operators 17
long int type 3
Loop breaking 34
Loop-control variables 28
Loops 27

M
Machine code 1
Mode in file operations 70
main() function 2, 15
malloc() function 41
math.h header 55
Mathematical functions ... 55
Modifiers 3
Memory
  address 6, 15, 20, 41
Modulus 11, 16
MS-DOS 1, 7
Multidimensional arrays ... 49
Multiplication 11

N

Nested loops 32
Newline escape sequence 14
NOT (||) logical operator .. 18
Numbers
   decimal 13
   hexadecimal 14
   octal 13
NULL character 14, 39

O

.OBJ files 8
Object
   code 1
   files 8
Octal numbers 13
Offset 80
Operators
   arithmetic 11
   bitwise 20
   combined 22
   decrement 19
   increment 18
   logical 17
   priority 11, 23
   redirection 71
   relational 17, 25
   replacement 12
   ternary 18
   unary 18
OR (||) logical operator 17
Overlays 47

P

Parameter declaration 59
Parentheses 2, 11, 23
Parenthesised operation .. 11
Pointers 39
   arrays 39
   arrays in functions 64
   file 69

   functions 62
   memory 41
   strings 39
   strings in functions 63
   structures 89
   variables 6
poly() function 55, 58
pow() function 55
pow10() function 55
printf() function 6, 12, 15
Priority 11, 23
Program flow 25
putc() function 71
putchar() function 16, 40
puts() function 39

Q

Qualifiers 3
Quotation marks 6

R

rand() function 55
Random access files .. 69, 80
Read file mode 70
Real variables 10
Records 89
Recursion 65
Redirection operators 71
Register variable 33
Relational operators .. 17, 25
remove() function 71
Replacement operator 12
return statement 59
rewind() function 71

S

scanf() function 6, 12, 15
Semicolon 2
Sequential files 69, 72
sin() function 55, 56
sinh() function 55

sizeof() function 42
Source program 1
Sorting 51
sqrt() function 55, 56
Standard arithmetic funct's 55
Statements 1, 2
stderr() function 71, 74
stdin() function 71, 74
stdio.h header 71
stdlib.h header 55
stdout() function 71, 74
strcat() function 47, 53
strcmp() function .. 44, 47, 53
strcpy() function 39, 53
strncat() function 47, 53
strncmp() function 47, 53
Streams 6, 69
String
   arrays 39, 43
   concatenation 47
   format 13, 15
   functions 52
   overlays 47
   pointers 39
string.h header 44
strlen() function 53
struct statement 90
Structure arrays 91
   linked lists 97
   unions 95
Subdirectories 8
Subscripted variables 49
Substrings 47
Subtraction 11
switch statement 35, 88

T
Tab escape sequence 14
tan() function 55, 56
tanh() function 55
TCC.EXE 7

Ternary operator 18
TLINK.EXE 7
tolower() function 78, 80
Turbo C compiler 7
Type variable
   conversion 4
   declaration 2, 50
   modifiers 3
typedef statement 87

U
Unary operators 18, 19
Unconditional branching .. 33
Underscore 3
union 95
unsigned types 3
User defined functions 59

V
Variable
   constants 5
   declaration 2
   double 3
   float 3
   floating point 10
   I/O types 13
   initialisation 5
   int 3
   global 59
   local 60
   names 3
   pointers 41
   real 10
   register 33
   type conversion 4
void 62

W
while loop 27
White space 6
Write file mode 70

COMPANION DISC TO THIS BOOK

This book contains many pages of file/program listings. There is no reason why you should spend many hours typing them into your computer, unless you wish to do so or need the practice.

The COMPANION DISC for this book comes with all the listings, organised into a separate subdirectory for each chapter. It is available in both 3.5-inch and 5.25-inch formats.

COMPANION DISCS for all books written by the same author(s) and published by BERNARD BABANI (publishing), are also available and are listed at the front of this book. Make sure you specify the BP book number and the book title in your order.

ORDERING INSTRUCTIONS

To obtain your copy of the disc companion, fill-in the order form below, enclose a cheque (payable to **P.R.M. Oliver**) or a postal order, and send it to the address given below.

Book No.	Book Name	Unit Price	Total Price
BP ___		£2.50	
BP ___		£2.50	
BP ___		£2.50	
Name .... Address		Sub-total	£.............
		P & P	£.... 0.45
		Total Due	£.............
Disc Format 3.5-inch....... 5.25-inch.......			
Send to: P.R.M. Oliver, CSM, Pool, Redruth, Cornwall, TR15 3SE			